SOMETHING WRITTEN IN THE ᴀRK

Keith Osborn was born and brought up in Wembley, North West London. He joined the National Youth Theatre in 1976, did one year of a physics degree at Bristol University 1978 to 1979 before going to Central School of Speech and Drama in 1980. He has worked extensively as an actor since 1983 during which time he also revisited his physics and mathematics career via The Open University graduating in 2000. He now lives in Alcester near Stratford-upon-Avon in Warwickshire.

KEITH OSBORN

SOMETHING WRITTEN IN THE STATE OF DENMARK

AN ACTOR'S YEAR WITH THE ROYAL SHAKESPEARE COMPANY

Foreword by Gregory Doran

OBERON BOOKS

LONDON

First published in 2010 by Oberon Books Ltd

521 Caledonian Road, London N7 9RH

Tel 020 7607 3637   Fax 020 7607 3629

e-mail: info@oberonbooks.com

www.oberonbooks.com

Cover photograph by Ellie Kurttz.

Photographs in text by Ellie Kurttz (237-252), Cressida Brown (244-245, 247), Gigi Buffington (248), Robert Curtis (247, 251), Steve Keeley (247), Keith Osborn (251)

ISBN: 978-1-84002-978-9

Printed in Great Britain by CPI Antony Rowe, Chippenham.

Contents

Foreword by Gregory Doran

IF you are lucky, you have an actor like Keith Osborn in your company; someone with weight and experience and staying power who can invest any role you give him with particularity and presence. In the 2008 ensemble (the "Blue Company") which I directed, he played Egeus, Hermia's splenetic father, for me in *A Midsummer Night's Dream*, but he also played a log in the forest; in *Hamlet*, Keith was a loyal Marcellus, trying to suppress his terror at the weird goings-on in Elsinore, and also sang the falsetto funeral dirge; and in *Love's Labour's Lost*, with only four lines, he delivered the pivotal moment of Marcade's arrival from the French Court with all the dignity of death. And he clog danced with a green face in the interval.

His blog, which he has here turned into a book, is just like Keith. It provides a thorough and telling insight into just what it is like being a member of the Royal Shakespeare Company, as he juggles the rigors of the rehearsal room with real life. He describes in often meticulous detail the process of rehearsal, and the stresses, strains and sheer hard work necessary to achieve the understudy requirement (Keith understudied Patrick Stewart as both the Ghost and Claudius). His days seem to be spent hammering up and down the M40 to London; snatching time with his wife Zoe, an ex-RSC Stage Manager herself, and Milly the boxer; ferrying his son Laurence back and forth from University; jamming with his ad hoc rock band; and worrying, once the season is all over, if he will ever work again.

Keith's book recounts a particularly happy company enjoying a season which, although happy too, was not without incident, as you will read.

Thanks and thanks and ever thanks ...

FIRST to Nada Zakula in the RSC press office who gently twisted my arm and persuaded me to find my inner blogger in the first place and whose help and advice was absolutely priceless in pulling together the key elements of this book especially the pictures, many of which David Howells trawled the RSC collection database for, way above and beyond the call of duty; many, many thanks to him also. On which subject special credit must go to Ellie Kurttz whose amazing production and rehearsal photographs, which feature within these pages continue to show her genius for capturing a magic moment in the blink of the shutter of her camera. Many thanks too to my Blue Company buddies Cressida Brown, Gigi Buffington, Rob Curtis, Kev Wimperis and also John Blizard who all allowed me to use their wonderful behind the scenes shots.

Thank you to Clea Boorman who read, and posted all my blogs onto the RSC website and for her endless encouragement of this novice writer, and to Kevin Wright for looking over and double-checking the text.

Thank you to all at The Shakespeare Birthplace Trust for access to the RSC production archives and the many show reports, rehearsal calls, meeting memos and more that were essential memory joggers, especially for the early part of this book.

Thank you John Wyver of Illuminations Media for some reminders of events on and off the film set of *Hamlet*.

Thanks to Oberon Books for running with the idea of this little tome, to Kate Longworth for her guidance and support, to James Illman for completing the jigsaw and making everything look beautiful and of course to Nick Asbury who trail-blazed the whole RSC blog-to-book thing with his brilliant *Exit Pursued by a Badger*.

Thank you Greg Doran for asking me to be a part of this amazing season, for writing the foreword and for his help in remembering things past.

To all my friends and colleagues in 'Blue Company' wasn't it a blast? And to everyone at the RSC who were integral to a fantastic season.

I want to thank everyone who read the original blog for all your kind comments whether via the website, by letter, card or meeting you face-to-face in the street or in the pub; I hope it gave some insight into an actor's life working at the RSC and if you are reading this, I hope you enjoy the latest incarnation of the story it told.

Finally thanks to Zoë for casting an eye over the text and putting me right on a couple of things, also her encouragement and patience over the months that I locked myself away at the top of the house to write this.

To my mum and dad
With whom it all started.

THE PROLOGUE

7th March 2008

FOR the past few months I've been working for one of the most important companies of its kind on earth. It has a massive, global profile, the work it does is sought by thousands the world over; today my job there has ended and I'm overjoyed! Fond farewells are said and good luck wishes exchanged with people I've grown to like very much and have had many a good time with. To my surprise and delight I even get a card and a couple of presents. As I leave the building for the last time I ask that rhetorical question addressed to self by so many actors, repeated mantra-like, ad nauseum, whenever a job finishes ... 'When will I be back? ... Will I ever be back? ... Will I ever work like this ever again?' The ambiguous answer to this is always '... maybe never ... MAYBE NEVER! This pleasing prospect fills my soul with warmth and I smile involuntarily. 'Nonsense, you probably will' growls the fiend on my left shoulder, instantly reminding me of the inevitable cycle of an actors life; I'm brought back down to earth, or indeed under the earth via the escalator at London Bridge Underground station, as I morph into a minnow caught in the overwhelming tide of the rush-hour crush of The Tube. But as I descend into the underworld my soul lifts again as the angel on my *right* shoulder illuminates and exorcises the shadow of melancholy cast by the devil on my left, reminding me that – inevitable cycle or no inevitable cycle – for the next few months at least, and probably longer, I'll be turning my back on the routine work of a temp in the office of the major consultancy firm PricewaterhouseCoopers and should look forward to a triumphant return to the Royal Shakespeare Company starting rehearsals the week after next; from PwC to RSC, from spreadsheets to Shakespeare, hurrah! And so it is with a sense of coiled excitement that I jostle along in the current with my fellow minnows heading

north from London Bridge to Marylebone to catch the
six o'clock back to Warwickshire ... blessed home ...

I first heard rumours about the particular season
I was about to be a part of via another Keith – Keith
Lovell, one of the senior dressers at the RSC – over
a year ago during *The Complete Works* festival in
2006. That season was an absolute triumph, so
many wonderful companies from all over the world
converging on the small market town of Stratford-
Upon-Avon where the son of a glove maker was
improbably born, survived the plague, pestilence and
cold winters of Elizabethan England as a child, and
came to man's estate to reach out and touch the hearts
of millions from all walks of life, from every continent
on the globe across time and space. That season I
played Agrippa in *Antony and Cleopatra* (directed by
Gregory Doran) and Decius Brutus in *Julius Caesar*
(directed by Sean Holmes), and one evening during
a performance of the former I was enjoying the usual
chat and banter in the hinterland that was the old
Back Dock joining The Swan theatre and main house
backstage areas in the old RST. The Back Dock was
a legendary, surreal place, a crossover region where,
since The Swan opened in 1987, casts and staffs (stage
managers, dressers, wardrobe and wigs etc) of the
two different shows in performance on a particular
evening would meet, and mutually impossible universes
would mix and mingle. A common sight that season
would be armour-clad Roman soldiers and members of
Cleopatra's Egyptian court in their flowing gossamer
robes, Planet Earth circa 50 BC, passing the time of day
with the 20th-century Sicilian villagers that populated
the world of Nancy Meckler's production of *Romeo and
Juliet*. It's funny but despite the fact that there were
other parts of the building where such incongruous
congress would occur (the green room, dressing

rooms, corridors), here the proximity to each playing area and the consequent adrenalin-fuelled sense of suspension one felt in the limbo between performance and non-performance lent an atmosphere that made this particular part of the building very special. The beloved Back Dock was thus a very fertile ground, indeed a veritable Nile delta, for humour and gossip, and as utterly amazing as the new building promises to be it will be much missed. Anyway, one such night during a break between scenes Keith and I were chatting and he told me that he had heard tell that Greg's 2005 production of *A Midsummer Night's Dream* was to be revived for The Courtyard Theatre in 2008 and furthermore that David Tennant was temporarily relinquishing his time lord status as The Doctor in *Dr Who* to become the eponymous Prince of Denmark in *Hamlet* and Berowne, that witty, caustic, critic at the court of Ferdinand the King of Navarre, in *Love's Labour's Lost*. Naturally this was of great interest to me, and anyone else listening, for although we were still mid-season, and temporarily well out of reach of the cold waters of unemployment, in the certainty that at some point the tug of that tide would surely come, my actor's instinct for survival compelled me to make a mental note of this potentially valuable piece of intelligence and file it for use at a later date.

After Stratford we took our shows to America – Ann Arbor in Michigan – and the Novello Theatre in London. On the 17th February 2007 I donned my splendid Roman armour for the very last time; whilst Rupert Goold's production of *The Tempest* was to start its run the week after, for me the excitement of the international stage of the RSC was over. I had been very interested in the 2007 season immediately following and actually met with Conall Morrison who was to direct *Macbeth*, but it was not to be. My

beautiful armour was swapped for the 'smart-casual'
weeds of modern office life, and for the time being my
blood chilled as I was drawn inexorably into that cool
current ...

Although my wife Zoë and I had bought a house in
Warwickshire just before the end of the London run, I
needed to maintain a London base as my son Laurence
lives with his mum in London. At that time he was in
the middle of his A-levels and I wanted to be around for
that. So through my invariably reliable source of temp
work I started immediately on Monday in London at
the major consultancy firm alluded to above; the first
of a string of temporary jobs that stretched through the
year. At that time Zoë was working as Stage Manager
for the magnificent *Histories,* which was about to start
rehearsing *Richard II* and the *Henry IVs* in London, so
at least we were there together for a bit. The pattern set
for both of us was London in the week and back to our
country residence at weekends.

In the weeks and months that followed I went to
auditions for various television and theatre roles and
did get a few little acting jobs that kept my hand in,
but nothing substantial. I was part of the RSC's Open
Day in April, some voice-over work in the summer,
a corporate video, a production of *A Soldier's Tale*
rehearsed, learnt and staged in a matter of hours for
a sort of mini-Glastonbury arts festival held in Sussex
that my friend and composer Stephen Warbeck runs in
June every year called 'Roger's Party'. Also an evening
of poetry about the Falklands War in 1982 at Warwick
University for which I was very excited to share a stage
with that iconic film actress Julie Christie.

The pattern of occasional acting work, temping
and the to and fro to London was disrupted when
the rains came and disaster struck. Our house is in
Alcester, a small town to the west of Stratford. We love

living there not least because apart from the fact that
Alcester is a gorgeous, historic Warwickshire town, our
house is right at its edge, with a beautiful view toward
Oversley Woods over verdant meadows through which
the Arrow and Alne rivers meet and wend southward
together. This blessing became a curse on the night of
Friday 20th July when along with thousands of others
in the United Kingdom, following the insane quantity
of rain that deluged much of the country, we were
flooded and consequently homeless for six months. I
was working in London for a travel company where the
weather had been very wet and that day there was a
particularly vicious shower of biblical proportions that
drenched one of my fellow office workers in a matter
of minutes, to all our amusements. But as the day went
on I became more concerned as the flood warnings
mounted and I received Zoë's periodic accounts of the
unbelievable, continuous rain in Warwickshire. She
was in the middle of technical rehearsals for *Henry IV
pt 2,* and against the odds I resolved to try and get back
that night. Chiltern Railways got me through the flood
as far as Leamington Spa and thence, brownie points
galore, they taxied us stricken passengers to wherever
we needed to get to. I met Zoë after she'd finished
her tech session that evening in The Dirty Duck (that
world-famous pub) at about 10:30 and we struggled
back to Alcester with our hearts in our mouths. At
times the road home ran like the rapids but somehow
we got back to see our house with the water lapping at
the doorstep. It became clear that emergency measures
were necessary and we started moving stuff upstairs.
Mark Graham, one of the production managers at
the RSC who lives in Alcester, turned up and climbed
through our window to help. Inevitably the waters
invaded the house, not under the door against which
sandbags and carpets were vainly stacked but by

snaking up through the stone floor as in some horror
film. We rescued the wine and retreated up the stairs
through our piled-up belongings and furniture to the
top floor to watch the water rise through the night.
In the morning we waded out in 3ft of cold water
with a couple of fearsome hangovers and for the next
months fell back on the generosity of Zoë's mum Janet,
becoming refugees in her house in Bearley nearby.

In the midst of this adversity Zoë continued to
mount the second *Histories* tetralogy in Stratford and
I yo-yoed up and down to London as time passed to do
temp jobs of varying interest ending back again at PwC.
In that time on the home front we tussled with loss
adjusters and insurance companies as we desperately
strove to facilitate the return to our new home as soon
as possible. On a brighter note we had an addition to
our family: Milly, the cutest little boxer puppy you ever
saw, so tiny tiny that she could curl up and fall asleep
on my shoulder!

Running through this period the information Keith
had disclosed the previous year in the limbo world
of the Back Dock became more and more concrete.
Through a variety of sources Dame Rumour gradually
fleshed out the picture of the forthcoming 2008 season;
Patrick Stewart was to play Claudius, Oliver Ford-
Davies Polonius, Penny Downie Gertrude. *Hamlet*
was to be modern dress, *Love's Labour's* Elizabethan.
Furthermore in addition to Greg's company there would
be another working in parallel on *The Merchant of
Venice, Taming of the Shrew* and some new plays. Dame
Rumour is a fickle friend but there's no denying that she
is powerfully compelling and, if nothing else, reminds
one to take action when the time is right. Summer
gave way to autumn gave way to winter, I gave way to
the melancholy borne of months of treading water, not
moving forward in my work and out of the house I'd

only moved into a few months ago; at these times one has to get really tough with oneself and INSIST that THIS TIME WILL PASS ... it will, it always does ...

In November I finally landed a proper acting job, an episode of *The Bill*. Perhaps, just perhaps, my luck was changing. This stirring of confidence reminded me that that next RSC season would be casting in earnest very soon, so I got my agent Sarah on the case with Sam Jones, the RSC's current casting director. For good measure I also wrote to her and sent Greg a card too. And then ... nothing ... Despite having been an actor for over a quarter of a century I can never quite get used to the fact that one tends not to get an instant response to any petition made for a job! I continually remind myself that this is extremely childish, if not paranoid, and one just has to be patient.

Over Christmas as Zoë's brother and his family were coming to stay with Janet, we were guinea pigs trying out a newly refurbished RSC flat opposite the old RST. That old familiar friend was no more, its belly ripped open to the sky by the demolition work that was well underway by now. Doorways opening out onto empty voids, the auditorium a tumble of seat and brick, the purple art deco interior flayed and spread to the grey sky, a wall of posters of past productions going back decades, torn and forlorn, open to the elements and the beloved back dock a pile of rubble. At this time, in my mind, this spectacle symbolised my own career – a pile of ashes and not a phoenix in sight.

New year came and at last, with it, the longed-for telephone call ... Sarah rang with the offer from the RSC while I was filming my *Bill* episode. How one call changes your life: one minute lost in the wilderness never to find the chosen path ever again, the next the prospect of a year's work with one of the greatest theatre companies in the world. Inevitably some negotiations followed regarding what principal roles, what understudy roles and what remuneration. All was agreed in a few days of to-ing and fro-ing; I was to play Egeus in *A Midsummer Night's Dream*, and Marcellus in *Hamlet*. At this stage there was some uncertainty as to what my role in *Love's Labour's Lost* would be, if anything at all. But all of this thus far was just fine and dandy and I could work the intervening six weeks at PwC, knowing that soon I would be back on track again.

Come February 2008 the laws of physics and the expertise of the builders decreed that our house was dry and mended and that we could return and relive the joy of when we first moved in exactly a year before to the day.

So, the final weeks in the realm of Tempdom have passed and I emerge from the subterranean universe of The Tube to scan the departure board at Marylebone for the platform of my departure from the shackles of spreadsheets, presentations, diary management and the rest. Within a minute I'm settled into my seat and the train pulls away from the confined carapace of the station roof to the limitless ultramarine blue of the early spring dusk to carry me home. A weight lifts from my shoulders, I breathe easy … just over a week to go and I start a great big brand new adventure … there is a world elsewhere!

Spring time the only pretty ring time ...

A play toward ...

THE spring morning sunshine fills my eyes as
I cycle down the Holloway Road for the first
working day of the season. The RSC has rehearsal
rooms in Clapham but at the moment these are fully
occupied by the *Merchant/Shrew*, or 'Green' company,
who are by now well into their own rehearsal period
having started back in January. This means that until
they leave for Stratford we will be setting up camp
for the first couple of weeks at The Union Chapel in
Islington. This beautiful Victorian, gothic church
is familiar to me because as well as being a striking
landmark it's a music venue; as a child my son,
Laurence, used to sing and play there in various local
choirs and orchestras, so I have a lot of affection for
the place. For years I've rented a room from one of my
very best friends, the actor and director Philip Franks
who lives in North London, so an added bonus of this
rehearsal venue is that I'm only a five-minute bike ride
away (cycling being my preferred mode of transport in
London) rather than the customary 18-mile round trip
to the RSC rehearsal rooms in South London.

Unaccustomed to the luxury of this short trip to
work I'm very early on this first day, and on a strange
impulse decide to get my hair cut. Being cranio-
crinigerously challenged ad extremis – oh all right ...
bald as a coot – this simply involves a few sweeps of
the electric cutters at minimum length setting and
I'm done. I don't know where this urge for a tonsorial
makeover came from, something to do with the new
start I expect. This takes the barber five minutes and
I'm on my way again to complete my journey to work.

The Union Chapel is a splendid church designed
by James Cubitt and completed in 1889, its 170-foot

tower visible at some distance over the surrounding buildings as I approach. The room we're using is at the back of the centrally-planned nave accessed via the road running behind the main building. I dismount and approach an anonymous wooden door. I'm about to meet the people I'll be living, breathing and working with for some time, and it's very exciting. I ring the bell and a disembodied voice I don't recognise squawks tinnily from a speaker embedded in the dark-stained brick wall asking what I want. 'I'm starting with the RSC today' and continue unnecessarily, 'we're rehearsing here.' ... pause ... 'OK, come in ...' The door mechanism buzzes open. I push the door and manoeuvre my bike through it in the hope that there'll be somewhere I can leave it inside the building. Animated chatter echoes around the dark corridor I'm standing in originating from beyond another door immediately to my right ... here we go, once more into the breech.

The room is big, high-ceilinged with a first-floor curtained gallery around two sides. About 30 people mill around the large space, my new workmates. There are quite a few familiar faces, people I've worked with before spanning the nearly three decades of my career, both older and newer acquaintances. Some I know well, others less so; I can't stop smiling. Greg comes over and welcomes me with a warm embrace and 'here we are again!' 'Well it's great to be here,' I reply. Greg and I go back quite a way and I've worked with him a lot over the last seven years. We first met in 1979 when I was at Bristol University studying physics (yes physics! I lasted a year before running away to the circus, but that's another story), and he was directing a student production of A Midsummer Night's Dream. As I remember he auditioned me for Lysander ... I think it was Lysander. Anyway I didn't get the part, but here I am now in this production 30 years later. Mark Hadfield is playing Puck, I worked with him at the RSC on the regional tour of 1987/88, when my friend/landlord Philip played Hamlet. Mark and I try to recall whether we've met since then and conclude that we haven't. Not all the connections are RSC-based: I also know Rod Smith because his daughter Sarah used to baby-sit for Laurence when he was a tiny dot; now she's 35 years old and an operations manager for a major retailer. My god where has that time gone! It has to be said that in the intervening 17 or 18 years Rod has hardly changed and, despite being slightly older than me – and possibly I am hyper-conscious on account of my newly shorn dome – I can't help but notice that he still has a very fine head of hair, the bastard! It's great to see more recent friends too: Peter de Jersey, Joe Dixon, Ewen Cummins and Mariah (Minnie) Gale, all whom I've acted with at the RSC with over the last few years, and the stage managers Suzi Blakey and Klare Rogers. Of course there are also quite a few brand-spanking new friends. Sam Alexander and I exchange greetings, we haven't actually met before but I was in the company with his dad Bruce Alexander in 1985/86, when Sam was about seven. I'm beginning to feel as old as the Union Chapel itself.

The effusive chatter of the new company meeting and greeting each other is brought to order by Greg, who welcomes everyone and summarises what we'll be doing over our first couple of weeks together. Then, as is common on first days, we play a few icebreaker games to try to get to know one other as soon as possible and begin the painful process of trying to learn, and remember, each other's names.

We stop after a bit and turn to view 'the model'. Basically this is made by the designer and is a scale model of what will eventually be the full-size set. Its

revealing is always a very exciting moment at the start
of work on a production – it usually sits, an enigma,
boxed up in the corner of the room antlered with angle-
poise lamps ready to illuminate the contents when
finally opened to scrutiny. It will be interesting to see
how the designer, Francis O'Connor, has adapted Greg's
original proscenium-arch production of *The Dream* for
the old now non-existent RST for the dynamic thrust
stage of The Courtyard Theatre. Ta-daaaa!!! The front
of the box comes off and collectively we lean forward
to inspect this representation of the physical life we
will all share for the coming months. The back wall
comprises a number of tall, vertical, mirrored panels
defining the upstage limit of the playing area. The floor
is made of shiny tiles about a yard square, mostly black
but with four clear ones forming the corners of a square
in the middle of the stage. Greg explains that this
simple, clean, shiny space will be the basis for all three
productions in our part of the Stratford season. Having
decided on what plays he would be directing he realised
that they are the three plays in the Shakespeare canon
that contain plays within plays – *Pyramus and Thisbe,*
The Murder of Gonzago and *The Nine Worthies* – and that
he wanted to explore an aesthetic that would resonate
with the convention of characters in a play watching
characters in a play. As the audience enter and take
their seats they will be confronted with a reflection of
themselves in a giant mirror held up to nature, thus
heightening their awareness of themselves as characters
in *real life* watching characters in a play. It sounds a
rather brilliant conceit and I'm sure it'll work well.
Francis then takes us through the elements of the set
exclusive to *Dream* that will define the three parallel
universes that make up the play: the Athenian court,
the mechanicals and the fairy kingdom, above which
the fairy king and queen will actually fly. These three

universes only interweave to comic and dramatic effect when civilisation is left behind in the wood without the town. However, the unifying element that is common to all set-wise is a huge moon (there's a lot of moon imagery in *Dream*) suspended high above the stage. This will traverse the playing space diagonally in real time through the first half, which should be fantastic. The viewing done, as is customary there is a round of applause and we break for a cup of tea.

In recent years it has been RSC practice to ease a new company into working together by including so-called 'training' sessions in the rehearsal time where various experts in often diverse fields are brought in to take sessions that directly and indirectly feed into the work we will be doing together. Whilst I'm not keen on the nomenclature ('training' makes us actors sound a little like dogs!) these sessions are invaluable in aiding and abetting company bonding. The first of these is a session on puppetry taken by Steve Tiplady of Little Angel Theatre company. Little Angel is a puppet theatre company based just down the road in Islington and Steve has brought his skills to the RSC before. On Dominic Cooke's 2003 production *Cymbeline*, which is where I first met him and a puppet version of *Venus and Adonis* adapted by Greg and first staged in 2004. He also worked on the last incarnation of this production, where puppets swell the fairy population and a beautiful toddler-sized puppet embodies the Indian 'Changeling' Boy, the struggle for whose soul is the source of the conflict between Oberon and Titania. The primer for we nascent puppeteers is to spend the rest of the morning finding objects that litter the rehearsal space and to transform them into puppets, and it's amazing to witness how, like some benign Frankenstein, Steve can animate and breathe life into a teapot or a piece of paper or a jumper. Fellow company member Sam Dutton is also an experienced puppeteer who I suspect will be charged with being puppet captain for the season to keep us all in line.

It's lunch and an opportunity to establish new relationships as people go off in small groups to forage for sustenance in the copious coffee bars and sandwich shops of Highbury.

When we return we start to read through the play. Stage management have arranged the tables in a large square as for an international summit, and we the delegates all sit round. In Greg's process this first work through the play involves reading each scene in turn round the table regardless of gender, BUT the golden rule is that no one is allowed to read or comment on their own part. First a section of Shakespeare's words are read out loud, then the reader has to paraphrase in their own – these are often very amusing. As well as the script itself, there are several annotated versions by various editors and dictionaries of Shakespeare's words scattered around the tables; a toolbox that helps us to unravel obscure meanings that crop up even in this relatively simple play. Also somewhere in the room there is always a printed copy of The First Folio, the closest we can possibly get to the original Shakespeare, which was compiled in 1623 by John Heminge and Henry Condell who had acted with him in the King's Men and to whom we must all be eternally grateful. Whilst the work of centuries of editors to unlock the meanings and lay bare the historical context of Shakespeare's poetry is undoubtedly a massive help in understanding it, sometimes you just need to get back to the source of the spring for a fresh look at what was originally set down. In The Folio, sometimes the way a line is split, an original spelling of a particular word, the inclusion or omission of a stage-direction will indicate alternative routes to those taken by editors through the ages.

We do this for the afternoon and then home ... that's it I'm off back to Warwickshire. No I haven't walked out or been sacked on my very first day, but tomorrow The Blue Company (our own official RSC colour-coding) is off en masse to Stratford to case the joint, hence I'm on my bike to Marylebone to catch the 6:30 and steal a night in my own house.

The Magical Mystery Tour ...

I T'S a building I've driven past countless times, but have never crossed the sacred threshold of; the RSC's Timothy's Bridge Road site. This fairly bog-standard-looking, large, warehouse-type building is the ultimate source of the RSC's home-grown sets, props, scene painting and a store for costumes old and new. Though not a flying buttress in sight, this banal exterior belies its status as a cathedral of the expertise that engenders the physical worlds you see on an RSC stage.

Despite still recovering from stage managing *The Glorious Moment* – where all eight plays in *The Histories* cycle were performed over four days from last Thursday to Sunday, concluding the Stratford part of that truly historic season – Zoë gamely gives me a lift in and drops me off, as I'll need to go back to London on the bus tonight for rehearsals tomorrow morning. I'm greeted by Suzi B our stage manager at the gates to this powerhouse of talent. The cast is crowded into the

small reception room supping tea and eating biccies
before being led by Michael Dembowicz, our company
manager, round the various departments.

First downstairs to the costume store, and there
are rows and rows of them from past productions.
Recycling Shakespearian Costumes is very common at
the RSC, some go back decades. I love old costumes.
Old costumes are often used in rehearsals to help actors
find the physical life of a role. Sometimes it's helpful
to throw off the everyday rehearsal room garb – more
often than not trainers, jeans, t-shirts and the like – and
swap it for weeds from an unfamiliar sartorial world.
Whether this be a pair of boots, a trenchcoat or an
Elizabethan dress, the donning of the right clothes can
release and give insight as to how a character may walk,
talk, breath or all three and more. I'm always curious as
to the individual history of a given costume, and more
than slightly obsessively like to check the provenance of
each one on the rehearsal room rail, reading the name
label inside to see who wore it and what in. Here at
TBR there are hundreds suspended in limbo, waiting to
be worn in earnest again, including some of mine.

We are ushered around the various domains of the
building, each of which have their own sense and
scale: the paint shop, where huge frames and stage flats
tower over us; the place where props are made; the
concentrated hush of the Drawing Office where stage
and set plans are drawn; and the smell of timber and
lightning flashes of welding in the scenic and metal
workshops, where the final touches to the set of *The
Merchant of Venice* are being made in anticipation of its
technical week.

We emerge blinking into the daylight and for the
next stop on our magical mystery tour we board the
bus and proceed to The Courtyard Theatre where we
will do some voice work with living legend Cis Berry.

Cis is a truly inspirational human being: now in her 80s she jets around the globe to work on voice and text with theatre companies the world over, and her approach has been core at the RSC for over 40 years. By means of physical exercises and ways of thinking and playing with Shakespeare's words she has developed an invaluable toolkit for actors enabling them to possess the text and make it their own. One aspect of this involves de-poeticising the words and responding to their raw sounds and rhythms so that their resonance and emotional power become greater than that flowing from an understanding of their literal meaning alone. This holistic approach to language enables the actor to engage with the text on all levels, mentally, physically and spiritually. An example of one of her exercises is that a sonnet or scene is chosen where one character is trying to communicate something important to another, and rather than be allowed to simply speak the speech he or she is physically restrained and dragged away from the recipient by the rest of the group. This means that the speaker has to overcome a physical obstacle and the need to communicate becomes more intense, the physical effort feeding the delivery of the words thus invariably attaining an earthy viscerality.

Its great to see Cis again and after a brief warm up we set to work on various bits of text. Cis's preferred method of distribution of the material for these sessions, the copies of these treasured and revered sonnets and speeches, is to throw the pages into the air in the middle of the group and for us to descend on them like seagulls foraging a rubbish tip in search of food, she exhorting us to be quick and get on with it with some good-humoured profanity or other. Cis has a wicked sense of humour, and as she moves amongst us her small frame belies the easy authority with which she commands these sessions.

The stage has been booked for exactly an hour and a half during a break in the dismantling of *The Histories* set, now well underway in anticipation of its move to London. Consequently we have to work around the various holes and bits and bobs that clutter the stage. This is a very exciting moment for me, as although I've stood on the deep thrust of The Courtyard playing area I've never performed here.

Next a late sandwich lunch in the upstairs foyer, and then we take it in turns to be measured. This necessary ritual happens early in rehearsal on every RSC season. Every actor is measured for the future costumes that will be found/made for him/her for each production. Hopefully these measurements will last the season BUT the so-called 'Stratford Spread' can strike, borne of the ease with which snacks can be purchased from the green room café and pints of ale from The Dirty Duck (that great institution of a watering hole frequented by actors in the company throughout the season. The wooden panels of the snug bar in The Duck are festooned with portrait photographs of those that have passed through its hallowed doors over many years. Some instantly recognisable: Laurence Olivier, Judi Dench, Ian Richardson, Michael Redgrave; others less well known and the subjects of oft-played guessing games over a post-show pint or two.) As a self-confessed lover of snacks, cakes and ale, I'm ashamed to say that I too have been a victim of the dreaded Spread. In 2003 I became increasingly mortified as my costumes for Greg's production of *Taming of The Shrew* got tighter and tighter – to the great amusement of my dresser – until the humiliation meant that I simply had to take my destiny into my own hands, go on a diet and join a gym! Anyway enough of that – I digress. These measurements are always taken early in rehearsal, and it's not just collar and shoe size: almost every section of every limb and torso is measured. Calf, thigh, bum, hand, forearm, chest, throat to waist, shoulder blade to shoulder blade, head, wrist, instep etc etc etc. This is so that, if necessary, a costume can be tailored precisely to each actor's physique.

I'm quite early on in the queue so once that's done I kill some time and go for a wander, then it's on the bus at 4:15 and back to London.

19th and 20th March

FOR each of these days before the long Easter weekend we start at 10:00 sharp for a vocal and physical warm-up. On the Wednesday we have an amazing session singing songs from Eastern Europe and Africa with Helen Chadwick. I've seen her group perform a couple of times and absolutely love this sort of stuff. For the rest of the day we continue text work with Greg. On Thursday we sing with Helen again and then another puppet session with Steve Tiplady. After lunch text work with Greg then a fascinating session on rhetoric taken by Benet Brandreth. These early days of rehearsal thus continue the Magical Mystery tour as, in addition to working through the play, we're exposed to skills and material that are unfamiliar. As well as nourishing the work this also helps to forge the friendships and bonds that are crucial to a happy and successful season.

25th-28th March

BACK after Easter for our last week at The Union Chapel. On Tuesday as well as for voice, movement and text we start work on the actual music for the play with Musical Director Julian Winn. The score for The Dream was written by Paul Englishby for Greg's last version of this production, (he's the composer for all three of the shows in our season) and whilst there may be some adjustments I suspect that it'll be largely unchanged.

Wednesday and we do some text work with actor/director Rob Clare who was in the year above me at Central School of Speech and Drama, work with Greg then an interesting talk on the play's imagery by David Wiles, particularly his theory that the play could have been written specifically for the wedding of Sir Thomas Berkeley and Elizabeth Carey. The latter was the granddaughter of Henry Hunsdon, the Lord Chamberlain for whose theatre company, The Lord Chamberlain's Men, Shakespeare was acting in and writing for.

Thursday, we do some mask work with Audrie Woodhouse of Trestle Theatre, and in the afternoon we're scheduled to have costume chats with Greg and Stephanie Arditti, the costume supervisor. Whilst we're remounting Greg's 2005 production for The Courtyard, significant elements of which will remain unchanged, Greg doesn't want to produce a carbon copy of the previous incarnation. He's sensitive to the fact that this time around a new group of actors will respond differently to the play and that any fresh ideas should not be stifled. An area where there could be some changes is that of costume. The show is set in modern dress but clearly it'd be unwise to try to shoehorn an actor into someone else's clothes, so this afternoon we discuss these in our various groups: Mechanicals, Fairies, Lovers and Palace Folk.

I'm involved in two of these subsets, as in addition to Egeus of the Athenian Court I'm also going to be a member of the fairy band. Fairy-wise, I'm more than happy to go along with the slightly sinister all-in-black look, and love the idea that the fairies aren't all pretty gossamer-clad sprites. As for Egeus I have the idea that he lives in the past, a reactionary, splenetic man who wields a brutal authority over his daughter Hermia (played by Kathryn Drysdale). And rather than the plain grey pinstripe suit worn by my predecessor, I propose that I'd like to wear a morning suit or similar old-fashioned look in contrast to the more modern suits of the younger folk. Whilst unsure about whether a morning suit would be quite right, perhaps too different to the others, Greg is open to the general idea of Egeus not being up with the latest haute couture, and so the dialogue will be continued; it is early days yet in The Magical Mystery Tour of rehearsals and the first tentative steps toward the finished production and all its elements are still being taken.

Way Down South

Monday 31st March

WE'VE left the northerly climes of Islington and have moved into the RSC's main London rehearsal rooms way down south in Clapham, which quadruples my round-trip to work every day. Ah well, it'll keep me fitter and provides a physical pre-warm-up for the regular 10:00 company warm-up if you see what I mean. The building itself used to be Clapham Public Hall and was built in 1911. It contains three large rehearsal rooms, one on each floor, a couple of rooms for wardrobe tucked away at the back in the basement, and a delightfully scruffy green room. It is one of those buildings that having been sporadically carved up over the years to suit different functions and is much like a super-terranean rabbit warren, with staircases and doors in unexpected places and circuitous routes needed to get from one place to another. When we finish here in four weeks it's gong to be refurbed, but I hope that some of its maze-like, scruffy charm will be preserved.

Today is the day of the read-through proper, straight through, each actor reading their own part and at last, having dissected the text in minute detail over the past two weeks around the table, this afternoon we start to rehearse on our feet for the first time.

As we might hope and expect, having gone through the text with an ultra-fine toothcomb the read-through goes well, and it's a wonderful moment to share the play in one chunk together for the first time and to gain a sense of its overall sound and shape.

Lunchtime and I set off to find my familiar haunts for sustenance. In Clapham one is spoilt for choice but over the years I've found myself to be a creature of habit in any given week, zigzagging across continents: vegetarian curry from India; back home for fish and chips; to Chinese and to West Indian cuisine; occasionally the expensive but delicious Italian delicatessen up near the Common. Whilst at this moment my diet is hardly slimming there tends to be no 'Clapham Spread', as I cycle about 18 miles a day to and from work.

After lunch we begin at Act 1 Scene 1 in which as Egeus I peevishly interrupt what Shakespeare sets up as an erotically charged pre-nuptial scene between the Duke of Athens Theseus (Rob Curtis) and the Amazonian Queen Hyppolyta (Riann Steele), with 'complaint against my child, my daughter Hermia'. It's a rubicon crossed to be on one's feet for the first time, slightly awkwardly juggling scripts (lines not yet learnt) and props. For this scene Greg wants me to have stolen a jewel box of Hermia's containing keepsakes from her lover. I like this idea very much, it tells a story of control and the invasion of Hermia's privacy as I spill the tender and intimate contents across the floor to be used in evidence against her betrothed Lysander (Tom Davey), whose sickeningly romantic poeticism I utterly despise. Egeus favours the conservative, smart, sensible Demetrius (Ed Bennett) as his daughter's future husband, and presents him to the Duke as an alternative and preferred candidate. As we play the scene in action we stop to discuss what we've done then go back and try new things; it's early days but at this stage important questions are asked, the answers to which will emerge in the coming weeks. Is Egeus serious about death being the price his daughter must pay for her disobedience? Why is Demetrius preferred to Lysander? Does Egeus harbour a latent homoerotic love for him? As a relative newcomer what does Hyppolyta make of the archaic penal code of the Athenian court? How does it affect her view of her husband-to-be Theseus who presides over such a regime?

In addition to the main call, in another of the rehearsal rooms we fairies start to work on the Changeling Boy with Steve Tiplady. The Changeling Boy is a beautiful object, a Bunraku puppet the size of a small toddler made by Lyndie Wright. Bunraku is a traditional Japanese style of puppetry in which the puppet is manipulated by means of thin rods attached to its limbs. The main puppeteer operates the head and right hand, a second one the body and left hand, and a third the feet and legs. Steve was telling us that in Japan it takes many years to master the legs before being promoted to the body and left hand, then even longer to get to be head puppeteer … and we've got five weeks!

In the voice room a dialect session with Majella Hurley for Andrea Harris (Titania), and at the end of the day a fight call for Riann and Rob with fight director Terry King for the very opening of the play; the RSC rehearsal process is starting to fire on all cylinders.

At the end of tomorrow's rehearsal is a meeting for the understudy company, which in these more enlightened times comprises most of the acting company. Following the introduction of the RSC's new understudy policy, gone are the days when relatively few actors had to cover all the roles for the entire season. I am slightly in limbo as it's still a little unclear as to exactly what it is I'll be doing understudywise. Certainly I was told that I'd be covering Patrick Stewart as Claudius and The Ghost in *Hamlet*, which whilst a fantastic challenge is in itself quite daunting, but what I'm meant to be doing in *Dream* or *LLL* is yet to be decided. I'm hoping not too much more, otherwise my season will be completely defined by understudy work … I'm sure all will become clear …

And it does … sort of … Cressida asks if I'll understudy Peter Quince in *Dream*. I'm a little chary of this given the Claudius challenge, but after some thought I agree that this'd be fun to do and not too onerous on the line-learning front. BUT I'm also asked if I'll be a walking understudy as Don Armado in *LLL*. I really hate to be a party-pooper, am all for doing the company thing and will absolutely do my bit to cover smaller roles in *Love's*, but really feel this is a big ask along with the others: it's not *huge* but it's a significant number of lines and a very tricky part. Also to be a 'walking' understudy is not even to appear in the play but spend it in the dressing room while everyone else has all the fun. We're talking in the stage management office at Clapham, also with Jim Arnold from the casting department. I can see their point of view as someone has to do it and it appears I'm the only one who can. Equally they can see mine in that taking Don Armado on with the other two will render my share of the overall understudy workload to be disproportionate. It's a perfectly friendly discussion and Cressida says that she'll have a word with Greg to see if they can shuffle the cards a little and find a way forward. The fiend on the left shoulder is back after several weeks absence with its weasel words. 'As far as the RSC is concerned all you appear to be useful for is understudying … you troublemaker!' I try and banish these irrational and baseless broodings but that evening I leave work feeling somewhat deflated, except, that is, for a small but fully inflated bubble of actor's paranoia at being badly thought of, 'difficult', not a team player. It's a bubble I determine to burst as I cycle home that evening.

Tuesday 1st April

OF course the bubble hasn't burst. I arrive at work still feeling pretty discombobulated. Then Suzi B tells me that Greg wants a little chat at lunchtime. Oh GOD!! What shall I say? I don't want to let the side down, and Greg is such a good man. I've known him a long time, he's given me a lot of great work and I don't want to make life difficult.

However Prince Paranoia must be banished as there's work to be done and it's a big day for fairies. Between the appearances of the characters of the Athenian Court in their scenes at the very beginning and then near the end of the play, my fellow courtiers and I are recruited into the fairy band (David Ajala, Sam Alexander, Rob Curtis, Sam Dutton, Minnie Gale, Riann Steele and Zoë Thorne). As I've already said this fairy world is not just populated by delicate little things but fairies of all shapes and sizes, which is just as well as I'm neither delicate nor little. We start to explore the specifics of the fairy scenes within the play and also how the fairy world operates independently of it, a fairy back-story if you will. Their hopes, fears, morality, what they make of the mortals that stumble into their wood, their relationships to each other, their king Oberon and his sidekick Puck (Peter de Jersey and Mark Hadfield), and the queen Titania (Andrea Harris). This may sound a trifle bonkers but it's important to do all this in order to make the fairy world REAL. We're not talking ultra-method acting here but we must create a fairy world that will seduce and capture the audience's imagination with its magic, otherwise we're just a bunch of actors prancing around in strange clothes and the story will lose its power.

As we all try to find our inner fairy, from the rehearsal room below we can hear the unmistakeable low, slow, elephantine … om … pom … om … pom … om … pom … of a tuba, which is a recording of the opening bars of Paul Englishby's music for the Bergamask dance that the mechanicals perform for the Athenians at the end and Mike Ashcroft (movement director) has started to choreograph. All the separate elements of the show are being rehearsed in every corner of this ex-Public Hall, I wonder what the original architects would have made of this usage.

Lunchtime comes and I loiter with intent as people grab bags and coats to see something of the outside world and seek nourishment. The room empties and Greg and I meet in the middle of the room. Smiling, he puts his arm around my shoulder and we wander away from the departing throng for our chat. 'Hmmm … we're overloading you a little aren't we' he says. I tell him my feelings and instantly realise how ridiculous

my overnight fears were; a solution has been found.
Greg tells me that Cressida'd been up into the early
hours and rejigged things so now Sam Dutton would be
asked to understudy the eccentric Spanish Don, which
is an absolutely inspired choice. I will play Marcade
in *LLL* and understudy Dull the constable. Marcade is
a part I'd mentioned to Greg in passing the other day
and although he only has a couple of lines, he also has
one of the most remarkable entrances in the canon. I
have fond memories of *LLL* as it's a play I did in my final
year at drama school, and the way the play turns on a
sixpence at the end when Marcade enters and delivers
his devastating news has always stuck in my head.
PHEW ... paranoid episode over and everyone's happy,
anticipation of a very exciting season back on track.

After rehearsal there's the understudy meeting I
can now attend to with a settled mind. The purpose
of this meeting (another regular fixture in the new
season timetable at the RSC) is to be briefed by the
assistant director and casting department on what the
understudy requirements are, to answer any questions
we might have and importantly to offer words of
reassurance and encouragement to those new to the
process who may be anxious about the task ahead.

Wednesday 2nd April   A LIGHT day for me today, an hour-long session
with voice placement Gigi Buffington who's come
all the way from Chicago to work with the company.

In the evening I go to see my son Laurence perform
his own songs at a gig in Kentish Town. The bar is
pretty crowded and he has a lot of mates in, most in
their final year at school. They chatter excitedly on the

brink of spreading their various wings and launching into the big wide world and I feel like Methuselah. His set goes well and I have a quick drink with him before he goes off into the night to some other corner of London nightlife – oh the energy of youth!

REHEARSALS in all departments again today including a sonnet session with John Barton. These sessions can be a little daunting as John can be brutally honest about whether or not one has rendered the piece convincingly, but he is a true master of the art and it's important not to take it personally because the notes he gives are invariably correct. He uses sonnets to explore technical aspects of Shakespeare's language and how these can inform the emotions. To this end we shouldn't regard the sonnet as reflective, a stand-alone poem expressing an internal dialogue, but a speech, an argument where the speaker is intending to affect and change a listener's point of view. John's and Cis's approaches are subtly different but complement each other perfectly; two sharp, distinct tools for the actor's toolbox.

Thursday 3rd April

WELL, we've managed to put the whole play on its feet as well as start to explore the puppetry, flying, singing and dancing elements integral to the production. Today the ass's head has arrived for Joe Dixon to try on for the first time; it was made for

Friday 4th April

Malcolm Storry to wear in 2005 so may need some adjustments.

As the train pulls out of Marylebone station and I return home for the weekend I reflect that all in all it's been a good week, a sound platform made from which to spring into action on Monday for the next stage of the work.

Halfway house ...

WE'VE had three weeks of our six week rehearsal period and have come a long way on our journey, but there's a long way yet to go. We're bonding well as a company and having sketched a rough shape of the play, now comes the devilish task of filling in the detail. So it's back to the beginning again, and as we know the play and each other better it's time to really get to grips with the characters and their relationships through the language of the play. Around these core rehearsal calls with Greg, those for dance, puppetry, singing, dialect etc continue to orbit, and this week Cressida will start to take understudy rehearsals.

Because of the self-contained nature of Egeus's scenes, although he's my principal role in the production I spend most rehearsal time in fairy mode, so after rehearsing the first scene in the morning I know that in all likelihood he won't appear again until the end of the week.

Late morning we work on with Paul and Julian on Paul's setting of the first fairy song 'Philomel'. Early afternoon, having already done some work with it, we really start to get to grips with The Changeling Boy with Steve and Mike.

We concentrate on the first confrontation between Titania and Oberon and work quite technically on how he'll be manipulated, by whom, how he gets on stage, what he does and how he responds to the conflict.

At the end of the day we join Greg's main rehearsal to show him what we've done, and he layers on the emotional direction of the scene: our fear of Oberon and his cohorts upon their arrival, his fury at Titania's insistence on keeping the child, and the argument that ensues between them. It proves quite tricky to ensure The Changeling Boy is visible to all on the thrust stage of The Courtyard, but we find a way and it's truly wonderful to see him start to come to life in our hands.

■

F IRST thing after the warm up we consolidate yesterday's work on the confrontation scene, then while the first encounter between Helena (Natalie Walter) and Demetrius (Ed Bennett) and Puck and Oberon is rehearsed we recap the singing of 'Philomel' with Julian and rejoin Greg to rehearse its staging just before lunch ... not a moment wasted during an RSC rehearsal period I can assure you.

Tuesday 8th April

In the afternoon the fairies gang up on Hermia and Lysander as they stumble aimlessly, lost in the wood. This is the first fairy/human encounter and whilst we're invisible to the humans as *fairies* we appear to them as fireflies to light their path and illuminate the grassy banks for them to sleep upon. Greg has the idea that we're intrigued by the strange ways of the human

species and comment to each other on the dialogue
between Hermia and Lysander before they fall asleep,
a little like the way people will chat about a television
programme as they're watching it. We not only work
on what the fairies say and how they say it, but also
take care to place our fairy whisperings so as to serve,
and not distract from, Shakespeare's text; hopefully it'll
amuse the audience too.

After tea we retire to the top room to work with
Steve on the moment following Bottom's entrance after
he's been transformed into an ass. Greg's idea here
is that the objects that The Mechanicals have been
using – teapots, toolbags, coats, chairs etc – take on
a life of their own, mischievously manipulated by the
fairy band in poltergeist mode, chasing the terrified
workmen from the scene and leaving Bottom alone to
wonder 'Why do they run away?' Also in Greg's original
production he wanted to include a short sequence to
start the second half as the audience were just settling
down, but first time around never had time to realise
it. This was for Snug the Joiner to come on stage with
his newspaper and Peter Quince with his bicycle,
both terrified and lost in the wood. Having witnessed
their lead actor's asinine metamorphosis and been
ferociously hunted down by their goods and chattels,
the nightmare continues as the bicycle dismantles itself
and turns into a monster and the newspaper refolds
itself into humanoid form to continue the pursuit –
leaving Oberon on stage to restart the show wondering
'if Titania be awaked'. I'm on bike duty and we begin
to play and to explore ideas. The wheels turning into
huge eyes, the bicycle pump a proboscis and the frame
the thorax of a giant wasp. Meanwhile the seat and
handlebars become the head of a bull à la Picasso and
the pedals its thundering hooves. Well it's a start.

We rejoin the main call at the end of the day and put together what we've done.

T HE process of side rehearsals, main rehearsal and assembly and consolidation continues. In addition today I have my first understudy rehearsal with Cressida and a costume fitting.

Cress and I talk through and read Quince's scenes. She tells me the ideas that've been discussed in rehearsal and floats some of her own, and thus we start the process whereby assistant director and actor must fulfil the objectives of the main production but inject a little of their own creativity as well.

I meet Stephanie in the fitting room in the afternoon to try on my scary fairy costume. Tom Hodgkins, who played Egeus/fairy before, is about my size and shape and I fit into his original costume – a thick, black fabric all-in-one jumpsuit type thingy with a bankrobber-esque fishnet stocking over my head for extra sinisterness. We don't have the footwear yet but that's being sorted. She's also brought something to try on for Egeus. Morning trousers, but an ordinary black blazer, waistcoat, collar and tie; the jacket is not the morning coat I'd first envisaged, but is a better choice. It looks severe and old-fashioned and different, just how I wanted it to, but isn't too far removed from what everyone else is wearing. For Egeus's appearance near the end of the play in the second half I try Tom's original green tweed, but it doesn't quite work for me so we decide that I'll wear a long Barbour-type wax coat over my suit. This feels good as he's not necessarily an outdoorsy type of guy and has hurriedly slung a coat

47

over his official clothes to try and keep up with the royal party on their wedding morning. Brilliant! It's very satisfying when the look of a character is agreed by all parties and works well.

The work goes on – as well as Egeus and fairy I'm stuffing understudy lines into my brain, have started learning the Bergamask dance, and by Friday to my amazement we've got through the play again … this is going far too smoothly!

Growing to a point

Monday 14th April

SOMEONE who has a deserved day off today is Mark Hadfield who ran the London Marathon yesterday to raise money for the Mental Health Foundation … for the rest of us its business as usual.

First thing, The Fairy Band explores the possibility of making forest noises live on stage rather than use a backing track. Sounds like a great idea and collectively we dive in to create an amazingly diverse sonic menagerie of forest fauna, with me offering my mosquito as just one specimen within it.

Now well into rehearsals and starting our third go through the play, today is the deadline for lines to be learnt and the intensity of the work ratchets up another notch. At this stage, liberated from carrying a script, actors become braver at trying things out. I did get a little carried away in the last rehearsal of the very first scene, in my volcanic Egean rage, I broke Hermia's keepsake box after hurling it to the ground and booting it and its tender contents of 'love-tokens' across the playing area as I rebuked Lysander he having

> ... *stolen th'impression of her fantasy*
> *With bracelets of thy hair, rings, gauds conceits,*
> *Knacks, trifles, nosegays, sweetmeats – messengers*
> *Of strong prevailment in unhardened youth ...*

Today I've been given a new one by Katie Hutcheson our Assistant Stage Manager and have promised to be more careful. I worry a little that my performance is getting a tad OTT, but Greg likes the anger, although I should explore more fully where it might come from. Perhaps Egeus is hurt at Hermia's striving for independence as she's no longer his little girl; a parental rite of passage I can identify with at the moment as mid-A-level revision my own son becomes more and more his own man. These thoughts about Egeus's anger get me thinking about Hermia later in the play when she also displays extreme anger at Helena's baiting of her in the big lovers' scene in Act 4; it hadn't occurred to me before but she really is a chip off the old block ... what brilliant writing.

At the end of the day we learn a new song, 'Glimmering Light', a setting of one of Oberon's speeches near the end of the play

> *Through the house give glimmering light*
> *By the dead and drowsy fire*
> *Every elf and fairy sprite*
> *Hop as light as bird from brier*
> *And this ditty after me*
> *Sing and dance it trippingly*

It's a haunting, beautiful melody and the idea is that eventually the whole company will sing it as a round perhaps scattered around the auditorium of The Courtyard.

Wednesday 16th April

MY fairy costume is finalised as I get fitted with a pair of heavy biker boots to complete the look ... no one's gonna mess with me in fairy land! There are wig fittings now, and Peter De Jersey and Andrea Harris disappear to another of their flying sessions with Gavin Marshall, the aerial choreographer, at the mysterious Caxton House in North London.

Friday 18th April

I HAVE my first dialect call with Majella Hurley on Friday. This is because Quince and most of the mechanicals are speaking in a West Midlands accent; in fact all the actors playing them are from the Midlands except Ricky Champ who's playing Snout the Tinker as an Essex boy. We have a good session and she gives me a CD to listen closely to, in order to help get the West Midland brogue thoroughly absorbed into my bloodstream.

On the rehearsal room noticeboard there's a note asking if anyone wants to be official blogger for the season. Hmmm ... I'll have a think about that.

Monday 21st April

THIS week is going to be VERY busy. As time has gone on the rehearsal calls have got more and more complicated with different priorities for each production element competing for time and space;

hats off to Suzi B for negotiating said calls' increasingly labyrinthine complexity.

First up we have another look at when Titania wakes up and falls in love with the ass-headed Bottom. For this sequence our fairy numbers are more than doubled by the inclusion of more puppets in the scene. Puppets have become a bit of a thing with Greg. In 2004 he collaborated with The Little Angel Puppet Theatre on a production of Shakespeare's narrative poem *Venus and Adonis*. It was remarkable to see how, despite being carved out of solid wood, the characters' facial expressions seemed to change as the puppeteers breathed life into them. Consequently Greg had thought that he might explore the use of puppets for the 2005 *A Midsummer Night's Dream*. Around that time he was helping his parents move from their family home in Cumbria to his brother's house. On emptying the attic he found an old pillowcase, inside of which was a collection of his sister's dolls. Inspiration struck and he asked her if she wanted to keep them. Her answer being in the negative the path was clear for them to find fame on the RST stage. To this end they've been suitably distressed and customised for the production; heads, bodies and limbs have been swapped around, black wings glued on, and they've been painted up to lend them the quality of wildness and danger that chimes with the overall fairy concept. At this point in the play, when summoned by Titania, rather than just run on we will appear instantly through trap doors in the stage. How we'll operate the traps with our respective dolly companions in hand isn't clear at this stage but I'm sure we'll find a way. There's also a notion that Bottom and Titania will be flown out, Bottom as in one of those old dockyard newsreels of donkeys being harnessed and lifted by crane to be loaded onto a ship, looking awkward and vulnerable, all sticky-out legs and ears.

The precise mechanics of all this will be worked out when we get to the technical rehearsal, which is now precisely two weeks away ...

■

Tuesday 22nd
to Thursday 24th

SUCH is the complexity of all the different calls we tend to do scenes out of sequence now. We rehearsed Act 4 and bits of Act 3 on Monday, Act 1 and bits of Act 2 on Tuesday, Act 3 on Wednesday, other bits of Act 3 and Act 5 on Thursday; everything is now growing to the point of a first stagger through of the play on Friday.

A bit of a hiccup is that Joe Dixon has fractured his left wrist and is in plaster from his elbow to his thumb. Not ideal at this stage of proceedings as he has a lot of complicated business to do as Bottom.

■

Friday 25th April

WE rehearse a couple of the set pieces in the morning in preparation for the stagger through in the afternoon. Basically a 'stagger through' – as opposed to a 'run through' – is when we play the play scene by scene in order but stopping between each to set up for the next. This reminds everyone of the play in its entirety, which we haven't shared since the read through several weeks ago now, and allows a collective surveying of the lie of the land before doing a full-on run through without stopping. It is one of my favourite points of the rehearsal process because you get to see all the work that your colleagues have done over the past weeks for the first time, and it is usually full of pleasant surprises.

I kick off proceedings with the rest of the Athenian court and the scene goes rather well. In Hermia's keepsake box, slightly naughtily, I've replaced the 'sweetmeat' chocolate heart we've decided on as one of the love tokens with a Cadbury's Crème Egg which gets a really good laugh when I hold it disapprovingly aloft on cue; I hope Greg buys the idea.

After the first scene, as I find my fairy, I note for the first time – despite the play being very familiar to me – that through the first act the location of the action of each scene becomes geographically more removed from the Athenian court. Shakespeare is moving the audience from the structured, authoritarian regime of the court, to the outskirts of the city and the domain of the mechanicals, to the anarchy of the wood where the normal rules of law, time and space no longer apply.

The stagger goes well and we're clearly in a good place at this stage. Some wonderful things already realised and other potential that will blossom over the final week and into the preview period. The Mechanicals' first scene, which I will watch closely from now on along with the other of Quince's scenes, is very funny, setting up the specifics of the individual relationships between them and the power struggle between Quince and Bottom very clearly. Mark Hadfield's Puck has a delightfully sinister edge but is also very moving as he is left alone when Oberon and Titania are reunited. The big lovers' scene is hilarious, as is *Pyramus and Thisbe* in Act 5.

A customary debrief after rehearsal in the pub and then I dash for my train home to Alcester for the weekend.

Saturday 26th April I HAVE new contact lenses fitted in time for the production week after next. Essential for me now: I'm only slightly short-sighted but stumbling around backstage in the dark without optical assistance has become progressively more hazardous over the past couple of years. I love wearing lenses, everything looks so much brighter and more shiny.

Monday 28th April REHEARSAL arrangements having peaked in their complexity last week, for this we're mostly all together again in one room pulling the threads of the production together for our last week in sunny Clapham. First thing: the warm up, which by this stage has become an opportunity to practise songs and dances rather than the more abstract vocal and physical exercises it has been hitherto. Today we concentrate on part one of the production. For the morning session we work through the notes that Greg has for us from Friday's stagger through, and run through the show up to the interval in the afternoon; at the moment this is planned to be after Bottom is led away to Titania's bower, or in our show hoisted heavenward.

A S with Monday, today we concentrate only on part two. Intriguingly Greg has a meeting with John Wyver of Illuminations Media and our own lead producer Denise Wood at lunchtime ... very interesting, is there something afoot we don't know about?

T HE day of our first run through and a landmark in any rehearsal process.

To make the best use of this crucial moment of truth we spend the morning 'topping and tailing', starting a scene then jumping to the end to work out how it can flow into the next as seamlessly as possible under rehearsal room conditions. It may seem extravagant to spend a whole morning doing this but it will enable a smooth run for us to get a closer sense of the rhythm and pulse of the show and thus what works really well and what might need rethinking.

A brief vocal warm up with Lyn Darnley (Head of Voice and Artist Development) after lunch and the room settles down for the afternoon's proceedings. Greg encourages those of us waiting in the proverbial wings to sit all around the mark up for The Courtyard stage, as well as out front, to remind those playing that a large proportion of the audience will be to the side of the thrust. A deep breath and off we go ...

The first run is a major leap forward from the stagger, more fine-tuning to be done tomorrow before the final rehearsal room run on Friday.

After the afternoon's run we have the understudy line run. Another fixed point in an RSC rehearsal calendar at which the understudy company get to speak all their lines together in preparation for working towards the understudy run proper that will be done after press night. Inevitably at this stage, especially having all worked so hard on the main production, some passages aren't quite embedded in the skull, but the vast majority are. This is good because you never know when you may be called upon and the first preview is but a week away now.

Thursday 1st May

MAYDAY! Mayday! The penultimate day in the rehearsal room. In the morning we do quite a bit of fairy work with the lovers and with Bottom. In the afternoon the rest of the company arrive and we continue fine-tuning.

Friday 2nd May

OUR last day in London.
We're not called until 11:30 so get a bit of a lie in. As a full company we practise the songs again, especially 'Glimmering Light', and then work sections of the play.

In the afternoon our second and last run through, and by this stage we're gagging to get out of the rehearsal room and into the theatre. For this run various members of the production team attend to take notes in preparation for the technical: where actors are standing for the lights, any quick changes for wardrobe or wigs etc. They don't tend to be the most responsive of audiences as they're all concentrating on their own jobs, but the feedback for the final run is excellent.

All that remains is for us all to share a glass of champagne, together to toast our efforts thus far. The bubbly is bought with the proceeds of Greg's infamous Mobile Phone Fund. This penal code is exacted such that if someone's mobile phone goes off in a normal rehearsal they are fined £5 and if, heavens forefend, during a run a whopping £25. The proceeds of the fines incurred by those sinners whose telecommunications equipment have thus transgressed buy the end-of-rehearsal libation we're currently enjoying. And so we say goodbye to what has been our home for the last five weeks and look forward to the next stage of our adventure together as we up sticks and head Stratfordward.

Stratford here we come!

T O welcome everyone to Stratford it's traditional that the Company Manager (Michael Dembowicz) hosts a drink for the new arrivals in The Dirty Duck on the Sunday evening before the tech. The pub buzzes with excitement as people touch base and swap notes on the new flats and cottages that will be their homes for the next six months, chatting and relaxing in anticipation of a busy week ahead.

Of course for me it's a return to base. Last weekend I didn't take the train but drove up to London, and yesterday I packed up most of my belongings from my

Sunday 4th May

room in Philip's house. It's a strange feeling moving out having lived with my good friend for most of the last 10 years, but with Laurence leaving school and hopefully taking up the place he's been offered at Oxford to study music, maintaining a London base is a luxury I can't afford at the moment. So fond farewells were exchanged although I'll definitely be back to pick up the rest of my stuff in the summer. I'm bound to be back in London at some point and there's every possibility that our season will transfer so hopefully my old room will be still be available. In any case Zoë will be staying there for the next couple of months as she's in London stage-managing *The Histories* at The Roundhouse; as is often the case with us, although we work for the same company we're often miles apart.

Monday 5th May

WE'RE not called until 1:00 pm for a health and safety chat with one of the theatre fireman and an orientation tour of The Courtyard building; how to find one's way around the various levels backstage and front of house. I set up camp in Dressing Room D with Rod Smith, Mark Hadfield, Jim Hooper and Ewen Cummins. There are five of us but it's quite roomy and near the stage, which is a big plus; one of the things I won't miss about the old RST are the stairs. Because we're all, of a certain age we decide to think of ourselves as occupying the Senior Common Room as opposed to the Junior Common Room upstairs occupied by the younger actors. The costumes are already on the rails on hangers, accessories in clear carrier bags and biker boots and smart shoes on the floor. Today is very light for most of us as the technicalities of the flying sequences are being put through their paces with the principal actors involved and their understudies. After lunch some have costume calls, and I have a wig call in the afternoon. Greg thought it'd be a good idea for Egeus to have a moustache, so we dig out a suitably Colonel Blimpish style of facial hair for my upper lip which will add to the patriarchal look of the character.

TECHNICAL work on stage in the morning so again we're not called until the afternoon. There's quite a bit of hanging around during the three or four days of an RSC tech so it's vital to come to work equipped. Consequently books, newspapers, crosswords, guitars and laptops add to the clutter of the dressing rooms. Today the fairies that have been allocated radio mikes are called first for a sound check of 'Philomel' with the band, and the tech starts in earnest at 4:00 pm.

Tuesday 6th May

The costumes look amazing; inevitably some are not quite finished but the parallel worlds of court, mechanicals, and fairies are perfectly delineated. I'm very happy with my cozzie. The black blazer, morning trousers, collar, tie, badge of office and my new moustache donned I feel Egeus-ly old fashioned, perplexed and cross.

I make my way to the stage, check where my first entrance is and generally get a feel for the dimly lit geography of backstage. Katie shows me where Hermia's box of tender treasures is and I check the contents: cards, billets doux, bracelet of hair, a feather, framed picture, cute little white rabbit toy and chocolate heart (Greg didn't buy the Cadbury's Crème Egg idea … bah!). The set is fantastic, the small model of card and paper we saw seven weeks ago now realised in full-scale. The monumental mirrors at the back of the stage stretch from the shiny black tiled floor to high up into the grid, from where a myriad of domestic light bulbs and the giant red harvest moon that comprise the Athenian heavens hang down over the playing area.

I love techs. In some ways they're a bit of a breather for the actors as the focus is on the mechanics of the production, meaning that the technicians and stage management teams take centre stage. We can step back a little and don't need to go full out unless to check a sound level, the timing of an entrance or a quick change. At the same time the performances that have evolved over the last six weeks are still slow-cooking inside. In fact technical rehearsals are long working days and involve a lot of stopping and starting and repetition, so to go full out risks getting completely knackered and incapable by the night of the first preview when with the inevitable uncertainty and nerves of the occasion you need to be in tip-top condition.

Techs always take a while to get going and then they find their own rhythm. Greg is particularly efficient at running them and I'm sure we'll get through this in good time. First off is for Terry King to check the opening fight. Opening fight? In *Midsummer Night's Dream*? In our version of this most well-known of The Bard's comedies first the lights dim to Paul Englishby's tribute to opening bars of Mendelssohn's famous incidental music, then the sequent clusters of sustained chords in the woodwind suddenly break into a dramatic fortissimo theme on brass and drums and the lights snap up on a fight with sword and shield between two helmeted and armoured combatants, at the end of which one is disarmed, forced to his knees and his helmet removed ... it is Duke Theseus! His adversary stands over him, sword poised for the *coup de grace*, promising an early night and off to the pub for all, and then ... she removes her helmet ... it is Hyppolita! At which point the betrothed royals dissolve into

laughter and start Shakespeare's text. It's an excellent
way of confounding the audience's expectations at the
beginning of the evening and sets up the feistiness of
Theseus and Hyppolita's relationship. But before Riann
and Rob can begin in earnest, it's necessary to adjust
the fight now that it's on stage and address any potential
extra hazards that arise in transferring it from the
rehearsal room to stage, like falling into the audience
for example. This takes a little time but we're soon up
and running into the first scene.

On my entrance, I storm in dragging Kathryn as
Hermia and hurl her across the stage as rehearsed.
Immediately I check with her that that she's happy with
that; she's wearing her proper costume heels now and
the stage is slippier than the rehearsal room floor we've
been used to. All is well, so moving swiftly on after my
brief exchange with Theseus I'm off into my big rant.
I don't go hammer and tongs yet, in tech mode I'm
checking how I can deliver it so that all sides and levels
of the audience get their share of Egeus's spleen. As I
remove the love-tokens from the box and throw them
on the stage I try to ensure they don't bounce around
everywhere, when I snap Hermia's necklace from her
neck this is done at first with care as I don't want to
punch poor Kathryn in the throat. And so the tech
continues for all of us, carefully feeling our way into the
action, making sure all is audible, visible and safe and
leaving any major acting aside for the moment.

On exiting from the first scene, we pause to see if
we're going back on anything. Suzi B says no, they're
carrying on, so off I trot to the dressing room to get into
my biker fairy costume; I don't anticipate getting back
to Egeus for a day or two. This is a quickish change but
I've established with my dresser, Michelle Davies, that
we don't need to do it in the quick change rooms or
backstage.

The rest of scene one is teched quite quickly as it's just dialogue between Lysander, Hermia and Helena, but the change into scene two is very complicated, as to create The Mechanicals' world there are quite large elements of set that they need to bring on to transform the clean geometry of the court into the cluttered interior of a large workshop in the suburbs of Athens: Flute the Bellows Mender brings on a welding cart; Snout the Tinker a hot-dog stall (with real hotdogs, oh what joy to an actor is the prospect of a practical hotdog in Act one!); Starveling the Tailor a sewing cart; all followed by Quince cycling on and leaping to turn on a large light bulb that has been flown into the centre of the stage. In addition David Ajala and Sam Dutton, who've quick-changed out of their court clothes, come on as road sweepers sweeping on a pile of filled black plastic bin bags, concealing Mark Hadfield as Puck who's dressed in a special coat made of bin bags so that he can magically appear in scene three to surprise and shock Minnie Gale when she enters as the First Fairy ... you can see it's all quite complicated, especially given the constraints of the vomitoria exits and entrances onto The Courtyard stage through the audience.

First the pure physical mechanics of getting everything on is practised until it's as smooth as can be for now (fine-tuning can be done later), then it is timed with the sound, lighting and music cues that cover the scene change. Once everything is on and cues synchronise as well as can be at the moment The Mechanicals pick through their first scene and any technical issues to do with personal props (poor Joe still coping with his wrist being in plaster) or blocking are addressed. And at the end of the scene everything has to come off again ... except Mark in his rubbish coat hiding amongst the bin bags, no doubt hoping the hot dog stall won't flatten him. So the process continues, and so we go through the play ...

The next couple of scenes set in the wood don't involve too much getting stuff on and off stage, and the effects are quite literally achieved with smoke and mirrors. Oberon enters dramatically for the confrontation with Titania through billows of smoke pumped on stage under the two central mirrors that have been slightly raised for that purpose, wheeled on on a skateboard-like contraption by his two hench-fairies, one of which is David Ajala who has now quick-changed from road sweeper to fairy. Technically we Titania-ites adapt the work we've done on manipulating the Changeling Boy for sightlines in the new space.

There is an effect in the next scene that I remember from when I saw the show in 2005. Puck returns after the first woodland scene between Demetrius and Helena, with the 'love-in-idleness' that Oberon has ordered him to fetch from the bank where the wild thyme grows, his arrival is heralded by a meteorite shooting across the night sky – back-projected on to the mirror – and a loud sound effect as he crashes to earth off stage. I remember thinking what a sophisticated, and presumably expensive, piece of computer-generated animation must've been required to make such a cosmic special effect. No such thing. The starry starry night sky is made with globules of coloured oil suspended in blue water in a shallow glass dish perched on an old-fashioned projector such as was new technology when I was at school; and the white track of the shooting star across the back is generated by Katie our ASM quickly sweeping her finger through the mixture ... eureka and hats off to some truly rough theatrical magic.

From tech to dress, from preview to press ...

S O ... steady as we go from Tuesday then into
Wednesday and Thursday of our technical rehearsal
and it's apparent that every cubic inch, every corner
of the stage out to the extremities of the auditorium,
from the lowest depths to the highest heights of The
Courtyard Theatre will be used for *The Dream*.

When during the Mechanicals' rehearsal in the wood
Bottom appears to them having been transformed
into an ass, in our production their collective terror is
compounded as we in the fairy posse chase them off
with monsters made of their own tools. Under the
tutorship of Steve Tiplady two saws and a carpenter's
bench are turned into a snapping wolf-like creature, a
glove and welders mask into a scuttling monster, and a
teapot and a coat into zombie. At the end of the chase
we run around the back of the audience to descend
sub-stage and take our positions to enter up through
the traps with Greg's sister's dollies. Sub-stage world
is very cramped; with just over a yard of headroom we
crawl through a maze of wiring, stage supports, pipes
etc to pick up our dollies and wait in pairs to spring
up through the four traps. The traps themselves are
made of perspex so those in the audience sitting in the
balconies will see us as shadowy figures lit from below
before we're summoned by Titania. It's a two-man
effort to open the diagonally-hinged tiles so my partner
in crime for this bit, Sam Dutton, releases the bolt and I
hold the piece to stop it swinging back until we're both
safely out. We join our fairy band members in the space
after Titania has called us and we reply:

Ready
  And I

> *And I*
> > *And I …*
> > > *Where shall we go?* SLAM!

And all four traps are slammed shut in unison after the end of the shared line

At the end of the scene Bottom and Titania are flown up, up and away. This took some working out technically and some cunning sleight of hand. Sam Alexander smuggles a nappy-like harness on stage for Bottom, on cue he slips it onto Joe from the front while behind I pass my dolly to Sam Dutton, grab the karabiner that has flown in from aloft, fasten to said nappy and hand it to Rob Curtis who takes charge of Bottom, while I help David Ajala clip the karabiner flown in for Andrea as Titania, at the end of which David and Rob check that all is safe – from stage to grid is about 40 feet and it's a long way to fall – and it's as simple as that. Our signal to Klare Roger the Deputy Stage Manager, who cues the flying, that all is well is simply for us all to move away and lie down on the stage to watch Fairy Queen and her genetically-modified ass-humanoid hybrid object of fancy levitate together for their cross-species tryst. As this happens all the lit bulbs that have been hanging over us descend in opposition to accentuate the upward distance travelled by the new lovers. Lights out and our cue to scurry offstage. Up I get and walk quickly toward the back and … BANG straight into the wretched mirror! In the semi-darkness I'd completely misjudged how far away it was, no lasting damage apart from feeling more than slightly foolish and being the butt of several jokes for the next half hour.

We got through the technical in good time for a dress rehearsal on Thursday evening. For me one of the tech's highlights was after I'd got back into my

Egeus costume in the second half for the scene where the lovers are found asleep. I'd wandered into the auditorium to see what was going on. Oberon and Titania had just been reunited and Titania preparing to take flight. This had been tried earlier and for a worrying moment Andrea had swept skyward and got caught up in the light bulbs. Anyway this had been sorted, and for the last few lines of their dialogue Peter De J led her by the hand in a circle around him. As she accelerated and her feet left the ground Paul's delicate orchestral and vocal soprano underscoring of the dawn chorus exploded into a rainbow of musical colour, the sumptuous chords swelled and Gemma Busfield's sublime soprano voice soared into the stratosphere, as Andrea spun aloft enveloped by the swirling vortex of her dress like a beautiful bird in flight … I was utterly gobsmacked at this magical confluence of music and action and my eyes welled up; a beautiful moment to be relived many times over the coming months and a marker to me at that moment that the show was going to work brilliantly in the new space.

The dress goes well on Thursday and we have a short notes session Friday morning and the luxury of a second dress in the afternoon so that things can be well prepared for the first preview this evening. Full wigs and make-up are *not* required for the afternoon run, which serves as an energised canter through the play, after a long week building up for the paying audience in the evening.

Pre-preview there's the fight call, and we in the fairy band establish singing 'Philomel' as our warm-up with Julian just after the half. We do this in the backstage area every night, each arriving at various stages of being clad, bewigged, made-up or all three for the show and it's a good moment to touch base before we face the multitude.

WELL, it went VERY well last night. First previews have their own energy and excitement and at Stratford some of the RSC's most loyal supporters tend to turn out for the occasion, which is a great way for the company to ease itself into a long run.

Very little went wrong which never ceases to amaze me given the complexity of these shows. We spend four days piecing together a giant jigsaw and then BANG we're doing it in front of 1000 people in a little under three hours (including interval). A smoke cue was a little late maybe, a prop left on stage, but best of all Rob Curtis running into the mirror on exiting at the end of the first half even harder than I did ... cruel I know but he was unhurt and we all found it childishly funny.

We have notes this morning and work bits with full technical back up in the afternoon then in the evening it's the second preview.

DAY off ... HUZZAH!

Monday 12th May to
Wednesday 14th May

WITH each preview the fine-tuning becomes finer. Performances honed, costumes adjusted, as are cues for lights, sound, music and set, all leading up to the press night when we will be set amongst the critics.

On Wednesday I'm called for an understudy costume fitting for Quince. I dump my stuff in the dressing room and make my way to wardrobe on Waterside. As I'm leaving the theatre a voice calls across The Courtyard foyer 'Keith, what about the blog?' It's Nada Zakula of the RSC press department. After having seen the notice in Clapham I had expressed an interest in being the company blogger, but what with the business of the last couple of weeks it had slipped my mind. 'Errmmm …' I demur … 'Oh go on!' 'Oh all right then!' Thus I'm quickly and easily persuaded to seal the deal. I've never written a blog before, or even read one, and wonder what on earth I should write about. Ah well we'll see …

After my fitting I go to the regular, new season meet-and-greet sandwich lunch with our co-workers at the RSC; those who work hard behind the scenes in the new offices at Chapel Lane in the Events, Finance, IT, Literary, Marketing, Press, Production, Sales and many other departments, enabling what goes on stage within this complex organisation. It's a small but important event – part of Michael Boyd's vision is that the concept of ensemble includes everyone in the organisation, not just the current acting company.

After lunch there's a photo call with the press. This is when the director chooses scenes that would make good material for the pictures that will appear in the newspapers locally and nationwide, and usually they involve people kissing or arguing. On these occasions the likelihood of one's visage making it to the national press can easily be gauged by the cicada-like T-KSSK, T-KSSK, T-KSSK, T-KSSK of the cameras fanned

around the stage, lenses glinting in the dark like eyes
in a peacock's tail. The intensity of this sound tends to
increase exponentially as the leading lady and gent's
lips touch or as the emotional temperature rises and,
hopefully, the pictorial results will help to sell the show.

Today is press day! Throughout the week the calls
have got later and today we have a gentle understudy
call with Cressida after lunch before a final company
session and warm up with Greg.

Between these final preparations and curtain
up some disappear for a nap, or at least some quiet
time away from the theatre; others go into a frenzy
of writing and distributing press night cards or gifts,
bought or homemade, which can show startling levels
of wit and ingenuity. Special mention should go to
Peter De Jersey who, whenever I've worked with him,
paints a watercolour cartoon card of each character
to give to each player, always capturing the conjoined
personalities of actor and role brilliantly and wittily! In
similar vein Greg usually gives cards sporting a print of
a Tony Sher original cartoon based on the production.
There's no way I can compete with either of those, but
I've found some fairy pens from a local shop to give to
everyone, which I hope people will find gently amusing.
I write the accompanying cards and then have a bite to
eat in the green room.

On the table in the corridor outside my dressing
room flowers bloom, bottles of champagne and
boxes of chocolates appear out of the air along with a
multiplicity of smartly wrapped presents and envelopes.
Likewise at the stage door which can resemble a mini
Kew Gardens.

All the pre-show calls go with an extra fizz; the vocal
warm up, fight call and we have an extra call for the 'up
and down' sequence where the two boys are physically
lifted and manipulated by us fairies for their love-in-

idleness drug induced 'cheek by jowl' pursuit and fight for Helena's hand just after the big lovers' scene. Final hugs and wishes of good luck as we gather backstage for our first press night of the season.

There is a fantastic response from the audience, a great party afterwards and a not-so-great hangover the next day before the next phase of the season.

Dream On

Saturday morning,
24th May

AT last we can say that our production of *A Midsummer Night's Dream* is well and truly on as of *yesterday*. Now, you may question that last statement, surely *The Dream* opened over a week ago didn't it? And you'd be right. What I allude to is that following our very successful press night and party, quite a few of us Dreamers had but the morning to nurse our hangovers before finishing work on the final piece of the jigsaw, The Understudy Run. There are understudies for nearly every role in every RSC production and a robust system operates to facilitate this stage of proceedings. For understudying doesn't only entail learning the principal's lines, but mounting a sort of mini-me, parallel-universe production in which every aspect of the main one must be achieved artistically and technically by the understudy actors, stage management and crew. This level of thoroughness is crucial because however well he/she knows her lines and moves, there may be fights to be fought, flying to be flown, puppets to puppeteer and this must seem as easy

to the understudy as to the principal actor to satisfy the
high expectations of an RSC audience, and of course
to be absolutely safe. We have had about five days to
re-mount a 10-person version of the full production
leading up to an in-house performance of the whole
play with all whistles and bells and as many colleagues
and friends as can make it to support as audience.

The necessity for understudies stems from the
statistical certainty that over the months, sometimes
years, of the lifespan of an RSC production someone at
some point will be ill or have an urgent family crisis to
deal with or be stuck on the M40 which means they are
'off'. I've been in many shows where an understudy has
had to stand in for the principal actor and one doesn't
necessarily get a lot of notice. In *Cymbeline* in 2003 the
actor playing Jupiter, the king of the gods, who appears
in a dream to Posthumous whilst he's in prison, was also
a soldier in the Romans v Britons battle scene. Having
thus strutted and fretted in stylised combat with shield
and gladius on the stage, he then had to sprint off,
run the length of the back dock and up several flights
of stairs to the very top of the Swan gallery, shedding
clothes and weapons as he went, to effect the quickest
of quick changes into Jupiter's flowing robes, crown and
wig, then to be lowered in a winged throne suspended
god-like in space above the stage to deliver a speech
of great profundity. One fateful night as he hared off
he tripped and smashed into a doorjamb. I saw him
stagger and turn, dazed and with blood streaming
from his nose, at which point his understudy, having
barely uttered 'Is James alri-?' was grabbed by the stage
manager, told: 'You're on!' and dragged aloft the Swan,
from where he was dangled 30 feet above the rest of us
on stage, his face still covered in woad, having been an
ancient Briton in the battle. From this highly exposed
vantage point, in his entirely understandable state of

discombobulation, he came up with a very interesting version of Jupiter's speech, which seemed to go round and round in circles forever. Fortunately we mortals below were dimly lit so our barely-suppressed giggles were easily hidden. Even shorter notice of 'You're on!' occurred more recently in *Antony and Cleopatra* in 2006 when the actor playing Pompey had forgotten that there was a Saturday matinee. Additionally, through some misunderstanding or other, he had been checked in at the stage door so no one had realised that he was actually 100 miles away in London. When it came to his first scene, the warlike beating of drums struck up, heralding the dramatic entrance of the mighty Pompey carrying a flame bowl as supplication to the gods flanked by his piratic cohorts, Menas and Menecrates. However on this occasion only the cohorts appeared. Backstage we watched speechless on the monitor as Menas, played by David Rubin, who was Pompey's understudy, with lightning wit spoke Pompey's first speeches as Menas in the full expectation that Pompey would appear in the next moment or two and the scene would continue as normal. As this expected appearance did not materialise, he had to continue referring to Pompey in the third person, which he did at first hesitantly:

Errm ... HE shall do well.
The people love HIM and ... errm the sea is HIS

As David spoke this he drifted upstage to the entrance door at the back of the Swan stage, only to be shoved straight back on by Alison Daniels the ASM with a hissed 'He's not here!' at which point, Menas instantly metamorphosed into Pompey himself continuing in the first person with gusto

MY powers are crescent, and MY auguring hope
Says it will come to the full

Hopefully the audience took this apparent attack
of schizophrenia to be an interesting gloss on the part
and an indication of Pompey's troubled state of mind.
The other piece of luck was that *David's* understudy
was his co-cohort (Ravi Aujla) who'd twigged what was
going on, gently segued from Menecrates to Menas
and the heroic duo finished the scene together. It
should be said that neither of the above is the norm,
and usually the state of play understudy-wise is known
before curtain up and can be a wonderfully exciting
experience, as I discovered when I had to go on as the
villainous Iachimo in the above-mentioned *Cymbeline*;
fortunately I was told at midday which was OK as I had
the afternoon to get my head together to tackle that
fantastic part.

Whenever an understudy goes on there is an
inevitable 'knock on' effect, a bit like the butterfly effect
in chaos theory (you know that thing where a butterfly
flaps its wings in Alaska and causes a hurricane in the
Caribbean). If an actor is off and an understudy is on
that means that usually the understudy's understudy
will have to go on, which means that the understudy's
understudy's understudy will have to go on, which
means that ... I think you get the idea. For example
in *The Dream*, if Joe Dixon is off as Bottom then Ricky
Champ (who plays Snout) goes on for him, this means
that Rob Curtis (playing Theseus) goes on for him
which means that Peter de Jersey plays both Theseus
and Oberon which means that someone else will have
to pick up some of Rob's fairy business, his share of the
puppetry, helping Titania into her bower and clipping
Bottom onto his flying line at the end of part one. Thus
a mechanical off in the suburbs of Athens would cause

a hurricane in fairyland. A solution has to be worked out for every possible eventuality; the Herculean task of solving the Rubik's Cubesque logistics of all this falls to our assistant director, Cressida, who is also responsible for taking the understudy rehearsals.

A key part of understudy rehearsals is to negotiate the tricky path of creating individual performances that also fulfil the requirements of the production. An understudy should neither simply reproduce a dead carbon copy of the principal's performance, nor divert too much from it such that it'd make no sense in the main production should they have to go on. So whilst we must enter and leave the stage as our principals do, rough hew their moves on stage and follow the overall emotional arc of the character in order to play with the other principal actors, Shakespeare, divine as his writing is, does give licence for the understudy to shape their own individual ends in the nuances of a part and make their own stamp.

Although we managed some in London and a little squeezed into the preview period, the greatest concentration of these rehearsals has been since press night.

Having rehearsed the understudy run in the rehearsal rooms and on stage when possible, in order for The Understudy Run to happen in the theatre it follows that we need to tech it, which we did on Thursday.

This is similar in purpose to the tech for the main production, but for this if more bodies are needed to set things in scenes etc, as this run is in-house stage management can help shift stuff. The tech goes well. Though there are *lightning* quick changes for Peter and Minnie Gale when they have to instantly transform from Oberon and Titania reunited to Theseus and Hyppolita on their wedding morning. If either have

to go on it's physically impossible for the action to
continue immediately as the latter pair enter as the
former exit, so should the need arise they won't be able
to fly out and the quick change will be covered by a
music cue to hold the audience's attention.

We had the actual run yesterday and it really
was a strange and entertaining beast, as it usually
is. With only *half* the company doing the *whole* play
inevitably compromises are made in order to for the
run to fulfil its purpose. The commonest of these is
when an actor is understudying two people in the
same scene, which may mean that he or she might
have to speak to themselves. For instance in our
version of *A Midsummer Night's Dream* Sam Dutton
is understudying Flute AND Starveling, so in the
understudy run a dextrous change of hat helped to
indicate which character was speaking. One of the
many good new things that Michael Boyd has heralded
in since becoming Artistic Director is that, as part of his
ensemble policy, as far as humanly possible *all* company
members contribute to the understudy process.
Before this, understudy companies tended to be much
smaller so you could have one actor playing three or
more people at once. When I did 'The Gunpowder'
season in 2005 there were only nine of us contracted
to understudy all the parts in the season, which was a
nightmare. Memorably in one scene in the understudy
run of *Thomas More* Peter Bramhill understudied
someone who was badly beaten up *as well* as the two
assailants. This meant that in the run he had to beat
himself up, which I have to say was absolutely hilarious;
to this day I think he holds the record for the most
understudy parts in a season – nearly 30 if my memory
serves me right. Fortunately that year company spirit
was such that a couple of the actors voluntarily took
on substantial understudy roles to ease our pain (three

cheers for Nigel Betts and Michael Jenn!). In reality the odds of all the actors understudied by one actor in a scene being off are slim so this wouldn't arise, however in that eventuality we'd have to think again ...

Anyway, after a week of hard work, including a couple of evening rehearsals when *The Merchant of Venice* was playing, the run itself went exceedingly well and I had great fun playing Quince. There was one potential disaster when in scene one Peter came on as Theseus and nearly disappeared down one of the traps as a bolt failed, which could've been very nasty. Obviously we had to stop while this was sorted and no doubt the mechanisms will be double-checked before tonight.

For now understudy rehearsals are over but of course that's not the end of it, we have to maintain the work we've done for the rest of the season. The next stop on our journey is Elsinore Castle and the imminent arrival of some new friends.

SUMMER'S LEASE

A Bit of a Break

SINCE last Friday's evening performance of *The Dream* we Dreamers've had six days off! This is a bit of a freak occurrence at this stage of the season but *Shrew* and *Merchant* have been on all week, the understudy rehearsals are done and we don't start *Hamlet* 'til Monday. Time to recharge the batteries and gird our loins before immersing ourselves in the greatest play ever written.

I've had a fairly lazy few days at home, did my own thing, cooked, caught up on some guitar practice, watched crap television etc. My son Laurence paid us a visit from London last weekend; he's revising for his A-levels and his Warwickshire pad serves as a place of calm for him to chill out and do a bit of reading without the distractions of the big city, well that's the theory anyway. Tuesday and Wednesday I had to go to Dudley. I'm doing a computer course at the moment to get a Microsoft qualification in the C# programming language. It's mostly distance learning but Tuesday and Wednesday I had an in-centre visit as part of the course. Why the hell am I doing a computer course? Well being a closet geek I do find that kind of thing quite interesting and have always had a penchant for science and logic. In fact – oh dear, confession time – I did physics and maths for my A-levels and intended to 'get a good degree behind me' before running away to the circus. However, it didn't quite work out like that: I went to Bristol University to do physics, dropped out after a year, auditioned for, and then went to the Central School of Speech and Drama. However, the circle was completed much later as I did a science degree with the Open University graduating in 2000.

Anyway I digress, basically the computer course is
because the slings and arrows of outrageous showbiz
mean that an alternative source of income is necessary
for most actors, and whilst I've been temping in
London when 'resting' I'm hoping to get higher-level
programming work that pays better when I return to
the all too frequently re-discovered bourn to which
most of us thespian travellers inevitably return. So as
and when, in a few months, if anyone needs a junior
programmer in C# and the .NET Framework do get in
touch.

Yesterday (Thursday), some family and friends paid a
visit and Friday I pottered about the house and took the
dog for a long walk. How the country has burgeoned in
this early summer especially after the rain; our young
boxer Milly loves the long meadow grass, running
through it with a truly Tigger-esque bouncing gait, her
back and head appearing and disappearing like some
terrestrial, canine dolphin as she moves through a sea
of buttercups, yellow and green. The smell of earth,
and grass, and blossom pervade the air. The lambs have
grown and populate the fields; we walk carefully by
and try not to panic them. Naturally she's on the lead
and is curious as to what these strange dog-but-not-
dog creatures are, as she is likewise with horses and
cows, though more cautious with the latter they being
much bigger than she. Warwickshire truly is a beautiful
county.

But tonight its time to go back to work, so into the
car and forth to the theatre for the evening show. I'm
looking forward to seeing everyone again and hearing
what they've done in their own times off. Six days is
not too long a break, but the first time back to a show
can be a little like returning to a road one has used
only once; the twists and turns of a relatively new

production are not yet hard-wired into one's brain and body and need to be carefully negotiated.

Saturday 31st may

IT was good to see everyone again looking rested and keen to get back to the show. The return performance went very well, although there were some problems with the set. Near the beginning of the play in the confrontation between Oberon and Titania, the huge reflective perspex screens suspended to make up the back wall suddenly acquired a life of their own and started thrashing around like things possessed making the most appalling rumble for quite a few seconds. As Oberon was berating Titania at the time it looked like he'd summoned up thunder and lightning to press home his point, so hopefully the audience just thought it was rather spectacular special effect, in fact the screens'd got caught on something and were the subject of much scrutiny by stage management and staff for the rest of the evening. To us on stage it was quite alarming especially as there was an accident last week in the changeover from *Dream* to *Merchant* when one of the screens came loose, fell and hit three of the crew. The demon screens misbehaved again near the end of the performance when, on being lifted and lowered again the middle ones, like things possessed, decided to hang at a worryingly rakish angle during the Pyramus and Thisbe play-within-a-play. Anyway we got through safely without any major disasters, the audience were very warm and responsive AND there was a do after hosted by National Farmers Union Mutual that sponsors much of the RSC's development work. They were good company and laid on a very flavoursome late supper for us.

What a bonus: free food + free drink = happy actors. A very civilised end to the evening!

■

Athens to Elsinore

Monday 2nd June

WE'RE about to start our first week's rehearsal for *Hamlet*. As a company we've bonded well over the last three months which makes starting the second show easier than the first; we've really got to know each other and polite conversation has given way to healthy banter and trust. But of course now we get to greet some new boys and girls. It was lovely to see Patrick Stewart again (who I worked with on *Antony and Cleopatra* last year), Oliver Ford-Davies (who I worked with at the Barbican over 20 years ago) and John Woodvine (I did the *Deep Blue Sea* with him in Edinburgh). I'd never met David Tennant or Penny Downie before, both of whom seem very nice, and there is an air of excitement and anticipation in the air as we all gather – ordinary mortals, Starship Captains of The Federation and Time Lords – for that first-day ritual of chat over cups of tea, coffee and biscuits before we venture into the rehearsal room for the first time.

Greg Doran is brilliant at first days, his intellect, passion and enthusiasm are infectious and he effortlessly rallies the company, setting us off on the road ahead and outlining how we'll start our journey.

The designer Rob Jones shows us a model of the set, which is beautiful. Again we have the mirrored back wall but this time with a twist. Quite literally a twist. As the audience enter they might be forgiven for thinking that they've come on the wrong night because at first glance the set is exactly the same as the one for *Dream* BUT these panels don't move up and down but turn round and round lending a completely different dynamic to the space. With this capability they can offer numerous entrances and exits, leading to secret chambers for Claudius and Polonius to hide behind to spy on Hamlet and Ophelia in the nunnery scene perhaps, or for Polonius to eavesdrop on the heated exchanged between Hamlet and his mother after the play scene. If they all turn ninety degrees the playing space almost doubles in size as the area upstage of the panel line becomes available perhaps for an army to march on the way to a little patch of ground or for Ophelia's funeral procession to appear out of the gloom beyond the panel line. I've alluded to the closet scene above, in our Elsinore Polonius hides behind a mirror rather than the arras in Shakespeare's text. Clearly he can't be stabbed through a mirror so Greg and Rob have had the idea that Hamlet shoots him with a pistol snatched from Gertrude's bedside table. As he does this a lamp is knocked over and in the blackout the panels turn unseen by the audience so that when the lights come up again a large bullet hole is revealed as the epicentre to a number of almighty cracks that spread radially across the previously glacial mirror surface, its rupture symbolising the splintering of the Danish court. It should be a real coup and we applaud appreciatively. There are some preliminary ideas for costumes to see, which are based on the styles of European royal families of the 19th and 20th centuries.

Greg talks about the various versions of *Hamlet*
from the so-called 'Bad Quarto', which is thought to
have been compiled by the actor who played Marcellus
(me!), to the First Folio. He also puts the stage history
in the context of the chain of Hamlets stretching from
Richard Burbage to the present day. There are various
editions of the play, pictures and reference books for
us to peruse. Then, in a departure from the norm,
Greg produces several boxes that contain what he calls
'props'. He dons a pair of purple rubber gloves, and
there is a moment of puzzlement. In fact the 'props'
are precious artefacts from the RSC's collection that
need careful handling. First he brings our attention to
two long, black, rectangular plastic boxes. The first of
these is opened and inside is Charles (son of Edmund)
Keane's sword that he used when he played Hamlet; it
is worryingly sharp. From the other he produces Henry
Irving's sword, which is blunted, made by Wilkinson
(yes THAT Wilkinson, where the razor blades come
from). These items start to bring home the real sense
of history that surrounds this play. There is more to
come as next Greg brings over a large cardboard box.
First he produces a small innocuous-looking lamp,
clearly very old, made of dark metal with thick green
glass lenses; apparently Henry Irving always kept it
with him. The rather grim details are that it turns out
he got it from a murderer who used it to illuminate
his crimes; whether whilst committing them or after
is not known. Greg reaches deeper into the box and
slowly produces a human skull, the skull of another
murderer that appeared as Yorick when Irving played
Hamlet; again it is clearly very old, the bone dark grey
with age. One more time Greg slowly reaches into the
box and carefully, brings out another skull, bigger than
the first, the bone whiter and obviously newer. It is the
skull of André Tchaikowsky, who died 26 June 1982.

He was a gifted pianist, composer and a passionate lover of Shakespeare who had seen many productions at Stratford; his recordings are still available and there is a website dedicated to him that tells his story more fully. André succumbed to stomach cancer aged just 46 and had bequeathed his skull to the RSC. When it was first handed over following the necessary paperwork, processing and cleaning it was still quite putrid so had to be aired in a bag on the roof of the old workshop building for two years before being in a fit state for storage. André had appeared on the poster for the Roger Rees's *Hamlet* in 1984, and nearly made it to the stage in Ron Daniel's 1989 production, but in the event a plastic cast of his skull was made and used instead. For most of the last 20 years he has languished in a wooden box, and now as the shadows flicker around the empty orbits of his eyes as if blinking on seeing the light of day for the first time in a long while, it is an odd, sobering moment. The proximity to our own time and the lack of anonymity stirs stronger feelings of empathy than for the first skull. And of course this is the heart of the play, the transient phenomenon that it is to be living, breathing sentient chunks of the universe. Hamlet meditates on this in his 'To be or not to be' speech and again, more viscerally, in addressing Yorick's skull in the graveyard, remembering him as 'a fellow of infinite jest' who had 'flashes of merriment … wont to set the table at a roar'. Here and now we are contemplating the skull of a brilliant musician that once contained the seat of his consciousness. He entertained many thousands of people, loved and was loved, started life in the Warsaw ghetto, travelled west via Paris to London where he settled to write and play and is now no longer with us. All being well Greg is hoping that in our own *Hamlet* André will have his RSC debut proper.

André and the other precious things are put back in their boxes to be returned to the archives, and we break for lunch. That afternoon we take a trip to the Shakespeare centre and are shown copies of The First Folio and the *Hamlet* quartos that they hold – again absolutely fascinating – and the obligatory group photo is taken.

■

Tuesday 3rd – Friday 6th June

FOR the most of the rest of the week, as for *The Dream*, we've been carefully unpicking the play to ensure we all know what we're on about in the simplest possible terms. As for *Dream* we go through *Hamlet* reading each scene in short sections, first in Shakespeare's then our own words. This part of the rehearsal process means a lot of sitting around. We actors tend to be practical people who are more comfortable in action, on our feet rather than just sitting and talking. That said this exercise is absolutely invaluable and well worth a few days spent rooted to our bottoms. Again no one is allowed to read or comment on their own role, which means that there is a collective sense of ownership of the ideas in the production, everyone having the opportunity to contribute to a shared understanding of the play regardless of the size of the part they're playing. I must say I enjoy this process of digging around a play immensely and nerdily arm myself with dictionaries and different editions of the text. It never ceases to amaze me how these plays travel with you through your life; different meanings emerge at different ages, and even having been in *Hamlet* three times (the first time being the RSC Regional Tour 1987/88), I still find myself surprised by what new stuff there is to be mined, either things that I've not noticed before or haven't fully understood. Apart from the sitting around the table bit, through the week there are of course the other hands-on, on-your-feet activities. The ongoing vocal and physical work we do as a company, and on one afternoon we split into groups to present our own playlets based on the 1st Player's speech relating Priam's murder, a passage Hamlet tells us in the play he chiefly loved.

After lunch on another day, as part of our esoteric, in-depth research, we settle down to watch a DVD of *Tales From The Public Domain*. Inevitably, bang on cue, the laptop crashes and I'm called upon as company geek to fix it, resisting the temptation to ask David T if he has a sonic screwdriver I could borrow. The iconic masterpiece that we are about to watch is a compendium of three classic tales and is actually an episode of *The Simpsons*, the *Do The Bard Man* section being a radical re-working of Shakespeare springing from Homer's telling the *Hamlet* story to Bart and Lisa. Bart is of course the eponymous Dane, Lisa Ophelia, Marge Gertrude and Homer Claudius. It was very funny and if we all end up wearing yellow make-up you'll know where the idea came from.

Up and Down, Up and Down

I T'S 10:35 at night as I motor away from Stratford, throttling up toward the M40. Small dark clouds are silhouetted against the deep-ultramarine glow of the last of the day to the northwest on my left. An unnaturally bright light in the sky catches my eye. It moves and is followed at some distance by another; fancifully I imagine an impending UFO invasion. But no, of course they are the bright headlights of the last aeroplanes heading in to land at Coventry Airport. I hit the motorway, now heading southwest down towards London and the blackness of the encroaching summer night, leaving the dying embers of day to flicker out behind me. The moon is high and looks with a watery eye, balefully staring down at the earth and the stars spark up one by one. The car lights of my fellow travellers form their own constellations that change shape with every second, bright red, flashing orange and white stars, comets and planets. We've just done *The Dream*, which is packed with celestial imagery, so I'm particularly alert to the contents of the night as I speed along. This late Saturday pelt down to London is one that many actors do as most are based there and want return to spend at least a day at home, before going back to their respective theatres on Monday. Stratford is relatively near but right now there'll be hundreds of us thundering down the darkening corridor of night on motorways from all corners of the country. For me this is in reverse: now being based in Warwickshire, I'm going from my home to pick up some stuff from my old London room; also I'm seeing Laurence for a mid-A-levels Sunday lunch.

I make good time and get back at 12:15 though of course I'm still buzzing from the journey so it's a glass of wine and the episode of Dr Who that has been recorded earlier in the evening before going to bed.

■

I'M up early-ish – for a Sunday – and have coffee and a chat with my housemates before loading the remnants of my London room into the car, which of course takes much longer than I thought it would. Finally it's done, I say my goodbyes (I'm not sure when I'll be back) and am off to meet Laurence. He's in good spirits, two exams down three to go. We go to a gourmet burger bar in Muswell Hill, near where he lives. Not exactly brain food but it's his call.

It's early evening, I'm in the car leaving The Big Smoke and returning home back up to Warwickshire. I don't mind driving in the day at least there's something to look at and I like to take the pretty route via Banbury over Edge Hill. The view of the Warwickshire plain from the crest is stunning – you get but a fleeting glimpse as the road swoops steeply down past Tysoe and Radway toward Stratford. Before I know it I'm back for a late dinner with Zoë and that's the weekend gone.

We're now at what you could call the second stage of rehearsal. Last week we had finished going through the whole play as a group, culminating with a cracking read-through on Friday, all and sundry mightily relieved to be permitted to read their own role at last. David in particular, must've been straining at the leash to get stuck into the most challenging of Shakespearean roles. It's nice to see that he and the other newcomers to the Blue Company family are settling in well. I think we original Dreamers have made them welcome, it really is a lovely company – one of, if not THE best I've worked with. As for Friday's *Hamlet* read-through interestingly, given the respective lengths of each play, it was only 16 minutes longer than that of *The Dream*.

THIS week we go through each scene with just the actors involved and talk in greater detail with each other, the director and assistant director, about how we may play them together. I play Marcellus who along with fellow-soldier Barnado has seen the dreaded sight of the apparition of Hamlet's dead father going by the watch with martial stalk on the battlements of Elsinore castle. He brings Horatio to the battlements to witness its anticipated third appearance. We discuss exactly who these soldiers are and their relationship to Francisco, a third soldier, whose watch Barnado is relieving. Questions are begged: does Francisco know about the ghost? From his point of view, why have we brought Horatio, a civilian, up to the battlements? When The Ghost appears, what is it? What is its effect on us? Also, theatrically, how can we freak the audience out when we come to do the scene in the theatre? At this stage we are still somewhat rooted to our bottoms, but this forensic dissection of the scenes in such depth without worrying about where we move etc will bear fruit and free us up to experiment and play when rehearsing in action on our feet next week.

For the first stage of the rehearsal period the whole company were called practically all the time to share these first responses to the play, but now we're often free for some parts of the day. Today I've got all afternoon off so drive back home to Alcester to return

Monday 16th, Tuesday 17th June

for the evening show; a sort of mini-London up and down.

Similarly on Tuesday, in the morning down to Stratford, the afternoon back up home, then down again for the evening. Although I've indicated that I've had two afternoons off, that isn't *quite* true. I'm understudying Claudius, which seems to be a much bigger part than I remember. This is partly because in our production Greg wanted Patrick to double Claudius and Old Hamlet. I'm keen to get the lines under my belt asap so have spent a good few hours buried in my script on both afternoons. The road to Alcester was once a Roman road, so it is quite narrow and straight. I really miss riding my bike – my main mode of transport in London – but the A46 is just too fast and dangerous for a wimp like me, let alone the daily challenge of Red Hill. This forms a natural barrier between Stratford and Alcester, offering a long gradual leg-muscle-eroding climb out of the former and a vicious steep muscle-tearing climb the other way. Of course riding a bike in London isn't the pleasantest of experiences either what with the fumes, taxi drivers, bendy buses and other vehicular hazards not to mention pedestrians who seem to think that being on a mobile phone imbues them with some form of superpower enabling them to just step off the kerb at no danger to themselves or me! But the 9 miles to and from rehearsals in Clapham kept me fit and I'm anxious to avoid that dreaded Stratford Spread. Algebraically speaking:

18 miles round trip + cycle = fitness (London)

But:

12 mile round trip + car + snacks from the green room+ beer in the Dirty Duck = ginormous stomach (Stratford)

Chastened by the *Taming of the Shrew* 2003 experience I'm quite careful about what I eat (or try to be). Luckily as I have to drive home now a single beer after the show is the only option, and of course there's walkies with Milly the dog too.

MIDSUMMER Day and it's double *Merchant* and no rehearsals. So it's more heavy-duty line bashing in the morning. I decided to take a break early afternoon and, being a lover of music of most kinds, just had to take a stroll round Alcester to check out the yearly Folk Festival… oh yes there was a beer festival too (didn't I mention that?) which meant that my good dietary intentions were suspended for an hour or two. Morris dancers were out in strength in the street strutting their stuff, and I spent some time in The Hollybush listening to people singing and playing guitars, accordions and drinking some SUPERB beer poured straight from the barrel. I mean the delicious nectar that is warm, still English beer fresh from the tap, drawn by the force of gravity alone.

With an iron will I resisted the sore temptation to make an afternoon of it, because guess what, it's back to the script again.

Saturday 21st June

Walking before we can run

A T last we're at the stage of rehearsals immediately post-text-work. It's always a great relief to be able to run around, wave ones arms about and do some acting. Marcellus appears at the very beginning so I was amongst the first to start the journey across the undiscovered country that is the physical life of our production of the play. Having dissected this scene round the table we now reassemble it in physical form. Francisco (Rob Curtis) is the first character on stage discovered by Barnado with the question that echoes through the entire play – 'Who's there?' We realise that the scenario with which the play *Hamlet* starts is already an extraordinary one in that Francisco, being the one on guard, is the one who should ask the question, *not* Barnado who is taking over. Thus Shakespeare immediately ratchets up the tension in this out-of-joint world. Marcellus and Horatio come into the scene, Marcellus asks Francisco who has taken his place; on confirmation that it is Barnado, as planned, Francisco is dismissed but … has he seen the ghost? Why does he seem so frightened? The language is fractured, edgy.

To kick off, we start to imagine what it's like to be in pitch darkness in the freezing cold in a remote part of a castle waiting for a ghost that may or may not be an evil spirit, and when it appears how that might affect the characters physically and emotionally. As 21st century actors we continually need to remind ourselves that the people in Shakespeare's world really believed in ghosts, witches and the like and that these metaphysical beings could bring great harm; our task is to make those fears as real to ourselves and thus gain the empathy of the audience. Our rehearsal room is big and very light and it's impossible to black out the windows in the high ceiling, which means that rehearsing this scene takes quite a leap of our imaginations.

In these early rehearsals we arrive at physical shapes for the scenes that are rough-hewn and unfixed. Over the weeks we shape them more precisely to how we will eventually perform them, although unless there is a technical reason for precise 'blocking' – like needing to be at a certain place on the stage to be lit or some such – there's usually room for change even in performance; when a company is working well together there's always scope to experiment and surprise each other with new moves and nuances to character. Obviously this must be within reason; for instance it'd probably be a bad idea if on impulse one night I decided that Marcellus spoke with a squeaky high voice, or suddenly developed a severe limp. Any variations to the scene played live should spring from what happens in the moment between the actors and the audience. Anything else should be discussed first – needless to say we haven't yet discussed the squeaky voice or the limp.

NOT called today and no evening show so head in script again in the morning. Alison Bomber of the voice department is taking a voluntary singing session at lunchtime. She teaches the most wonderful choral folksongs from all over the world, their complex harmonies swoop from dissonance to assonance, they are fantastically uplifting to sing and clear my head for the afternoons homework. As I'm leaving the rehearsal room I note with interest that there's a flying call at the theatre for David Ajala and Sam Dutton; I think it's for the dumb show before the famous play scene

Tuesday 24th June

where Hamlet tests Claudius, which we're rehearsing tomorrow. Back home in the afternoon, more understudy lines ... I counted them and there's over 500 ...

Wednesday 25th June FIRST off, voice call with Lyn. Rehearse play scene in the morning, home for more Claudius cramming, show in evening.

Thursday 26th June GUESS what ... yep, head in script in the morning. *Dream* matinee in the afternoon.

Friday 27th June ONE aspect of the physical life of a play for which there's no room for experiment or improvisation are fight scenes.

The fights in the graveyard and in the final scene between Laertes and Hamlet are major set pieces in the play. Ed Bennett (Laertes) and David have been working on the core of these with the fight director (Terry King) for some time. This morning the rest of us, the Danish court, are fed into these scenes and a first draft of our involvement as spectators and combatants is sketched out. Structurally the graveyard fight is an untidy and macabre scrap over the corpse of Ophelia, and in the final scene a fencing match that gets wilder and more out of control as it evolves, with catastrophic consequences.

One of the things we've decided is that Marcellus is head of security at Elsinore and has been Hamlet's bodyguard along with Ewen as Barnado. We're both fed into the fights in both scenes to try to protect the prince and separate him from Laertes. The priority in any stage fight is safety, absolutely above and beyond everything else and *especially* when there are swords involved. It's just fisticuffs in the graveyard, which is still potentially dangerous, not least because when we come to do it in the show there'll be a gaping hole in the stage waiting to swallow some unfortunate actor up if they're not careful. In the last scene rapiers are the weapons of choice and whilst they are blunted they could still hurt or even blind someone. There are strict principles for approaching a fight. At first the moves are choreographed in short sections, dead slow, with exacting precision. Holds and punches are pulled, and sword points don't cross in front of anyone's face even if they're not directly involved in the action. In addition to getting a broken nose or blinded there's the possibility of collisions, furniture knocked flying and hitting folk, falling off the edge of the stage, tripping over stuff on the floor and the list goes on. To obviate *any* risk of injury from *any* source this process is followed again and again gradually building up speed and energy over weeks. Even when the show's up and running, as a matter of course in any production there's always a fight call to go through the moves before every single performance.

It's a good morning's work on the fights and David and Ed have done sterling work on the duel. At lunchtime there's an Artists' Forum meeting. Essentially this is a channel of communication through which the actors and stage management meet the producers (Denise Wood is ours as well as Lead Producer at the RSC) so that any issues affecting the current ensemble can be addressed. This is another recent innovation which I'm pleased to say isn't just a talking shop and was instrumental in evolving the new understudy policy.

Afternoon, home, understudy studying ... WHEN WILL THOSE LINES SINK IN? I'm finding Claudius significantly harder to learn than Old Hamlet. Old Hamlet's language is rich and complex, but he speaks in no uncertain terms, from the shoulder. He's an old soldier, a man of action who 'smote the sledded polacks on the ice'. Conversely Claudius is a man who uses words as weapons, he wouldn't dream of smoting anyone. He doesn't mobilise an army but sends his emissaries with letters to enlist the support of Old Norway in the suppression of Fortinbras's potential threat. That said it is clear that Denmark is covertly in a state of military preparation at the very top of the play with the daily casting of 'brazen cannon' and 'foreign mart for implements of war'; but these activities are secret, hidden as Claudius's true nature is. In reflection of this his language is convoluted, ambiguous, political. I wonder how the two brothers played when they were boys. It's a fascinating twinning of roles; it's a long season and I *could* go on for Patrick, hence I must not only be word-perfect but also really get behind these diametrically opposed mindsets.

Words, words, words – a letter of contrition

DEAR Readers,
Having dedicated some portion of the last chapter to the culmination of the understudy process for *Dream*, and my loquacious articulations of the same for *Hamlet* over the last few days, I hereby promise that I won't go on at length on the subject of the 'U' word any more. However … having been buried in my script for almost every free hour, minute, nanosecond of my free time over the last week I beg your indulgence one last time. You may have gathered that I've found myself getting into a bit of a panic re. Claudius, which as I write this I've spent longer studying than my principal role Marcellus. The thing is, quite apart from the *contractual* requirement to be word-perfect by the first preview (24 July), what if Patrick is – heaven forbid – incapacitated, or his car breaks down, or whatever? I'LL BE ON THAT'S WHAT! In front of 1000 paying members of the public, a fair proportion of who I guarantee will be profoundly disappointed that Patrick is off and whose expectations will be very high indeed; I've really got to be on the money for this one.

The weekend of June 28th and June 29th amid more line-learning

Learning lines when you're actually playing the part is much easier than understudying it for several reasons. Obviously you have hours of rehearsal to get to grips with it, as opposed to whatever time the assistant director can filch from the main schedule. But also when rehearsing you get to associate physical actions and moves with the lines which help them to fuse with the cerebral cortex. As an understudy, lines are learnt in isolation, the actor alone with his script, at home or on the way to work, in shops or the Post Office, or wandering the streets. To that end it's a question of repetition, repetition, repetition of small chunks of speeches, then on to whole speeches, then whole scenes one by one until the whole play is built up incrementally in ones head. Then back to the beginning again, then again, then again, then again ...

Although the language is difficult, Shakespeare's verse helps in several ways. The rhythm of the iambic pentameter itself (de-DUM de-DUM de-DUM de-DUM de-DUM) can act as a hook to catch those elusive words and meanings. Also whatever internal rhymes, alliterations or antitheses can be found help too.

Basically, magpie-like, you steal whatever tool you can to burn the lines into the synapses. At some point, you think 'phew, it's all in there, HURRAH!' BUT in rehearsals on your feet more often than not even this relatively mild performance pressure means that what's been rock solid in your bonce whilst on your own in the comfort of your armchair, with a beverage of choice, turns to complete slush in front of your fellow understudies. With inexorable cruelty the lines melt like snowballs in the sun – or the hell of your own paranoia – as you conclude that THEY'LL NEVER SINK IN! Of course eventually they do but boy oh boy oh boy sometimes it feels like they just won't.

So readers all, it remains for me to offer my sincere apologies for the subject matter of this missive. I can assure you that I fully intend that it'll never ever happen again. And also to reassure you that if you see a bald man answering my description wandering the streets of Stratford or its environs in an apparent state of agitation muttering under his breath about ambition, poison or murder worry not ... it's probably me.

Yours faithfully,

K

Running after we can walk ...

LATE morning we recap the fight work we did on Friday and Greg layers on the acting and reactions of the court to the extraordinary climax of the play, which sees the entire Danish court wiped out in a matter of minutes and the entrance of Fortinbras who, in true Shakespearean fashion, fills the power vacuum and restores order. Greg is unsure as to how we show this, or even if we need to. In our script the play finishes with Horatio's heartbreaking farewell to his dead friend. The English Ambassador who appears in Shakespeare's text with news of Rosencrantz and Guildenstern's death is definitely dead and buried, but at this stage Greg's unsure as to whether should we include the political context provided by Fortinbras. The debate will continue.

In the evening we actually start understudy rehearsals from the top of the play with me as the ghost not saying a word ... so no worries with the lines there then!

TODAY as an experiment we rehearse all the battlement scenes on The Courtyard Theatre stage in complete darkness with just a couple of torches for light. Greg has had an idea that this'd be a really good way of opening the production; it proves to be a very fruitful exercise. After the brightness of the rehearsal room, it was surprising how being shrouded in darkness pierced only by the narrow cones of torchlight added to the mystery of the first scene and made us feel quite jumpy; Patrick's first and subsequent appearances were genuinely startling. We're working to try and find a way of distracting the audience with the torches to give the illusion that the ghost just appears in the middle of the stage from nowhere. Also at the end of the scene we want the ghost to appear in several places at the same time. To this end Greg has the idea of using decoy ghosts for which Ryan Gage, Sam Alexander and Rod Smith have been recruited to be disguised to look like Patrick and lend a further feeling of dislocation of time and space to the scene. To our surprise and delight we also discover how useful the reflective surface of the stage is to bounce light around the playing space; what a coup for actor power … quite literally.

Wednesday 2nd July

WE work the complex final scene again in the morning and in the afternoon we in the military have a session with some real soldiers from the Warwickshire Territorial Army. We practise drill and also the protocols of how we greet and behave toward each other when on high alert, in which warlike state Shakespeare tells us Denmark is in at the beginning of the play. It's all good stuff and really adds a rigour and specificity to our military codes of conduct.

W E rehearse the play scene in the morning. The players, 'coted' by Rosencrantz and Guildenstern for Hamlet's entertainment, have been rehearsing the dumb show and the play-within-the-play proper in camera with Mike Ashcroft our movement director, and we in the court can't wait to see what they've been up to. It's quite something. The dumb show is grotesquely expressionistic; the characters communicate in a raucous semblance of speech, their movements are exaggerated, cartoon-like and it's VERY funny; Jim Hooper is outrageous as the Player Queen as is Sam Dutton as the Player King, appearing from beneath her skirts upon which she offers him her breasts, which he promptly buries his face in. The action is deliberately provocative, crude and crazy and done this way solves a conundrum that's always bothered me about this bit of the action – why doesn't King Claudius stop the dumb show that so clearly implicates him in regicide? While in this version when the Dumb-show murderer pours poison into the Player King's ear it may be obvious and unsettling to Claudius what's going on, the characterisations are so outlandish that it's not at all obvious to the rest of the court so the King realises he can let it run. After the Grotowskian dumb show *The Murder of Gonzago* couldn't be a greater contrast. Rod Smith introduces John Woodvine and Ryan Gage as the king and queen who enter very formally. Through this, Greg wants the discomfort of the court to become increasingly obvious as the action goes on, so when Ryan as Player Queen says:

> *In second husband let me be accurst!*
> *None wed the second but who killed the first.*

It lands like a bomb in the middle of the room. The tension is ratcheted up until Hamlet's interruption and the exit of the King. Patrick has had a great idea, rather than fleeing in panic on 'Give me some light! Away!' which is what usually happens, he rises as indicated in the text. He walks calmly through the players, asks for the lantern that Lucianus is holding with the first part of the line and illuminates Hamlet's face, eyeballing him as if to say 'I know what you're up to', exiting calmly on 'Away!' It's a very powerful moment and he's definitely on to something.

I'm THRILLED to have a singing call with John Woolf in the afternoon. A couple of weeks ago I half-jokingly suggested to Paul Englishby that Marcellus should sing a countertenor lament at Ophelia's funeral as part of the procession. I hadn't really thought about it since but it looks like it might happen. John tells me that Paul has suggested it to Greg and he's interested in the idea although it's not set in stone yet. Anyway Paul has written a devastatingly beautiful Miserere, the searing arc of which I find so emotionally engaging that for this first session I just keep choking up with emotion. As I've got older I've found that music moves me far more than it ever did whether listening to, or singing, or playing it. From experience I know that with practise I'll soon be able to control my feelings and channel them into the song, but it's quite freaky at this early stage. The Miserere is technically difficult, and there are long, high, sustained notes that must sound effortless and ethereal requiring precise breath control. I'm out of my comfort zone. I can tell there's a lot of work to do but am up for the challenge and am really chuffed and grateful to Paul for entrusting it to me.

In the evening the company are invited to a showing of Anthony Sher's film *Murder Most Foul*, a documentary about the kidnap and brutal murder of Brett Goldin and Richard Bloom in Cape Town in 2006. Brett Goldin was a talented young actor who was to've

played Guildenstern in the Baxter Theatre production
of *Hamlet* directed by Janet Suzman that was part of
The Complete Works Festival in Stratford that year. I
remember well the shell-shocked company arriving in
Stratford just days after it had happened. Following this
dreadful event the RSC, The Baxter Theatre Company
and the Actors' Centre in Johannesburg set up a bursary
in his memory to enable young South African actors to
come to Stratford to work and train with the company.
We watch Tony's film with Thami Mbongo and Nick
Pauling who are the recipients of the bursary this year.
They have joined in with our voice and movement
classes, observed our rehearsals, sung with us, drunk
with us, taught us gumboot dancing and have been
great company. It's their last day tomorrow and we'll
miss them. There is a sombre mood after the film, and
I wonder how Thami and Nick felt watching it. The
film tells the story of that awful night with devastating
effectiveness and is a passionate indictment of the
terrible, mindless, random violence that wracks South
Africa today; no doubt in some part born of the violence
of the apartheid system that oppressed the majority of
its population for so long.

Not wanting to go straight home some of us decide
to go for a pint. I drive down to The Duck, and as I park
up between the pub and the RST I look back to see a
rainbow floating high in the Stratford sky, its graceful
arc framing the half-built, half-demolished theatre, its
transcendent beauty a symbol of hope, shimmering
brightly from the sorrow of the rain that caused it.

Friday 4th July

GREG further develops the detailed crowd work we made a start on the other day. First the graveyard scene, then we spend some time on the pursuit of Hamlet after the murder of Polonius. Another crowd element that Greg wants to try is for us to be the 'rabble' that follows Laertes' rebellion heard offstage behind the seats of The Courtyard, so we start to work on how that might work. To add to the emotional cruelty at this point of the play he also wants us to mock Ophelia just before her re-entrance into the mad scene when Laertes' day takes another turn for the worse.

Having decided to keep 'How all occasions to inform against me' in – there was some discussion as to whether this was just a reprise of 'O what a rogue and peasant slave am I' – we work with Mike Ashcroft on how 11 of us can represent 20,000 on the verge of imminent death 'to gain a little patch of ground' in the so-called 'Eggshells' scene (earlier on in rehearsal around the sitting-down stage, every scene was named in a way that somehow summed up its place in the play); and this time I don't think Greg has any plans for using puppets.

As for *Dream* every interstice of the rehearsal rooms is in use: voice calls with Lyn Darnley; text work with Rob Clare; singing with John; fighting with Terry. Fightwise, as well as the big set pieces we mustn't forget the smaller scuffles and tussles: every little moment of onstage violence must be carefully worked out for safety and believability. Today we work out the scuffle between Hamlet, Horatio and Marcellus. We've set the play in the 20th century so it's unlikely that Hamlet would carry a sword, yet he must have one on which he makes them swear an oath of secrecy when they catch up with him after his encounter with the ghost of his father. Greg solves this by David disarming me, of the dress sword I'll be wearing as Marcellus, while Peter and I grapple with him to try to stop him following the ghost.

A very busy day not ending until the end of our understudy call in the evening at 8:30, and we're in again tomorrow morning to rehearse the final scene again AND we have a show tomorrow night … it's tough at the top, but SO worth it.

T HE work trajectory now follows that well-trodden path as for *The Dream*. Back to the top of the play we worked through all the scenes once again one by one, our walk through each scene of the play accelerating to a jog through each act for each day of the week culminating in the first run on Friday. We also had costume fittings this week and some of us went to the sound department to record the rabble's shouts in support of Laertes' rebellion, to help lift the live noise we'll be making in the auditorium. In addition I had to do some recording for understudy purposes. In the play, when Hamlet swears Horatio and Marcellus to secrecy, the sound of Old Hamlet's voice booms from beneath the ground in support of his avenging son. But Greg wants this to crescendo with each intervention until the entire Courtyard is shaking to The Ghost's exhortation to 'SWEAR!' Patrick records his sequence then I mine, so if I have to go on as the ghost it'll be my voice thundering around the theatre at that point.

Time for the first run and here we are again. Until recently I haven't been in the main rehearsals as much as for *Dream* so it's with even more excitement that I look forward to a first sight of the complete picture – or

Week commencing
7th July

at the very least what I'm sure will be a very fine first outline – to seeing the shape of the play, and hearing how one scene chimes with another as the whole journey is undertaken. Inevitably as we're poised to start there's a frisson of uncertainty as to how it'll all hang together; however well rehearsals seem to've gone and even though we all know this is not the end product, the question hangs in the air as with every first run-through: are we on the right track or hopelessly lost?

In the event the run through was fantastic, by turns moving, disturbing, painful and sometimes very funny. It really is a wonderful play that turns on a sixpence. Greg was very pleased, there's fine work from all the company and David is going to be a brilliant Hamlet. The closet scene with Penny was very moving, as was Minnie as Ophelia in the mad scene, and Oliver's Polonius is as hilarious as Patrick's Claudius ruthlessly controlling. But as we all know very well the evolutionary process doesn't stop here. Nothing is fixed and our task now is to assess where we're at, what works and what doesn't, and what we will try and discover next.

Later that evening we were back to the warm sensuality of *Midsummer Night's Dream*, a welcome contrast to the chilly rottenness in the state of Denmark.

Sunday 13th July

TO round off the week, it's Patrick's birthday! He's invited me and some others in the cast to his beautiful house in Oxfordshire for a light lunch and drinks. It's a beautiful day and the drive from Stratford through the rolling hills of middle England, green turned gold in the summer sun, is a joy. He's a great host and we have a lovely afternoon relaxing in the sun

in his garden; what a wonderful way to unwind after
a long week as we gird our loins for the final week's
rehearsal …

STOP PRESS – Bits and bobs

H OW could I have forgotten one of the single
most important events in RSC life at the
moment, the development of the RST? Last Sunday
– 6th July or 'Site Sunday' – I donned a hard hat in order
to see the building works up close. Well, I wanted to
don a hard hat, but disappointingly for us adults only
children were actually allowed to wear one. I know
– bloody actors, always wanting to get a cozzy on – but
still, I ask you! It was quite an overcast showery day,
but there was a good turnout for the staff preview at
11:00 before the public viewing in the afternoon, which
was also well attended. Susie Sainsbury – our Deputy
Chairman of The Board – greeted us at the gate, clad in
a fluorescent working jacket, and we entered the site
via coffee and cake in the pre-fabricated contractors'
canteen. I think that the new theatre is going to be
absolutely amazing, but the last year has been tinged
with a little sadness with the demise of the old RST:
such a familiar landmark for so many years, host to so
many memories, now with a huge chunk bitten out of
it. I've described a moment in its disembowelment
when last winter the auditorium was demolished
and the old town-side dressing rooms, as tatty as they
were characterful, pulverised and turned to dust.

Now, however, the demolition phase is complete
and the rebuilding is well underway; the walls of the
new auditorium are already being constructed and
starting to show over the boundary fence. It was quite
disorientating standing inside the shell of the old RST,
of which only the listed foyer, the riverside wall and
the flytower survive (The Swan is untouched). Jagged
lines on bare brick walls trace old staircases like scars
and closed doors up high that now would open out to
vertiginous empty space are all that betray the old inner
structure. Standing amongst it all it's hard to work out
precisely where one is in relation to what was there
before. From the back of what were the stalls I look
out across at the old brick proscenium arch framing
the dark void that was the stage, gaping like a huge
toothless mouth beneath the cliff-like edifice of the
flytower, and a deep pit sunk into the ground where
the stage and the front of the auditorium were. The
extraordinary history of the RST was brought home
when in the old circle bar I met one of my current
dressing room buddies Jim Hooper, talking to John
Blizard who had been his dresser some years ago. John
had a grainy black and white photograph of himself
standing in the middle of Bancroft Gardens with the
RST clad in scaffolding behind him, a building site;
only *this* photograph must've been taken in about 1931
when John wasn't even two years old, and showed the
very building works that were now being demolished.
How heartening and exciting to think that now, 80
years later, for all the mud and shattered brick we are
at the very beginning of a new cycle in the life of the
building and the RSC.

We work very hard as a company and so I think
that it's important to have another interest during a
season in Stratford. One thing I always try to do if
at all possible is to form a band. As well as me there

are usually at least one or two budding rock stars in
the company, and I've managed to assemble some
form of beat combo several times in the past, with the
permutation of instruments and voices defined by who
can play what in the company in any particular season.
For instance, in 2002 (The Jacobethan season), it was
just Jamie Glover on guitar, me on bass, and one song
– appropriately enough – 'Two of Us' by Lennon and
McCartney. We sang in The Swan as part of a charity
gig and called ourselves The Bandog Governors ... don't
ask, it's a quote from *The Island Princess* by Fletcher.
2003 was a golden year, I managed to assemble a full
five-piece called the Aglet Babies – another quote (your
starter for ten: where from?). As well as some covers
there were some beautiful original songs by Esther
Ruth Elliott who was in that year's company. We played
at the RSC fringe festival AND the first night party of
Titus Andronicus. The last couple of times, seasons in
2005 and 2006, were less successful: for some reason
people just seemed to be too busy (where were their
priorities?!). This year however I scent success. At
the moment the core of the band is me on bass, Rod
Smith (mandolin), Sam Alexander (ukulele) and
Mark Hadfield (bongos and percussion), PLUS various
permutations of guitar and keyboards and whoever
fancies coming to sing with us. We've already got
several songs under our belt, an eclectic mix ranging
from George Formby's 'Leaning on the Lamp Post at
the Corner of the Street' to 'Pyscho-Killer' by Talking
Heads. I think we're going to call ourselves The Captain
of Our Fairy Band, or something based on a quote from
A Midsummer Night's Dream, *Hamlet* or *Love's Labour's
Lost*. Our manifesto is that if anyone in the company
wants to sing a song, we'll work it out and be their
backing band. We hope to do a little concert later in

the season when we're less busy, whenever THAT may be.

■

It's the Final Countdown!

AFTER Friday's run there was much food for thought. No doubt over the next week some ideas will be jettisoned, others developed further, and many new ones tried; at this stage the show is still growing and will continue to do so through previews, press night and beyond.

Monday was quite a big day for understudy rehearsals as Greg did a lot of work with David on his own and with Penny and Minnie so we were available to work with Cressida. I did some text work with Rob Clare and Lyn Darnley on Claudius, it's very useful having more than one perspective on how to approach Shakespeare: to unlock a particular speech we actors magpie-like steal whatever we can from whoever we can to help us achieve our ends.

Tuesday morning we worked on the big final and play scenes – in the morning, had a session with Cis on stage in the afternoon and worked the beginning of the play. At the end of Tuesday I had a costume fitting.

■

I HAVE a song call with John Woolf first thing. I've continued to work hard on the Miserere. I was, and am, quite daunted by it as I need to use a part of my voice that I don't use very often – the so-called 'head voice' or falsetto. I can sing but I'm a belter, and this song requires something much more delicate. It's very high in pitch, there are a couple of long delicate phrases that require precise breath control, so as well as my own resources I'm calling on John and Paul's expertise and also that of the voice department, Alison Bomber and Lyn Darnley, in order to do it justice.

We of the 11 going on 20,000-strong Norwegian army have a whistling rehearsal. Paul has written a brilliant parody of a marching song, it's a cross between 'The Great Escape' and 'Colonel Bogey', and the idea is that we will whistle as we march up and down in a blizzard upstage of the mirrors while Hamlet and the Captain contemplate the little patch of ground.

In the afternoon we run the play for a second time and take a huge leap forward. There's greater assurance as to its shape, giving us the confidence to be braver with everyone upping their game. Thursday we are all called to work notes arising out of Wednesday.

I HAVE a morning song call AGAIN. Hardly ideal as one's voice tends to warm up during the day, so first thing there's a bit more of a croak factor. What's extra daunting today is that I'm joining Paul's band call, so am feeling the pressure a bit singing in front of all the RSC musicians rather than just Paul or John. Fortunately my fears are unfounded and it goes just fine, in fact Jimmy Jones the percussionist is very complimentary later in the day which is praise indeed coming from a proper musician.

It's the final run through in the rehearsal room and we have the usual audience comprised mainly of the producer (Denise Wood), designer (Rob Jones) and technicians who will work on the show, on sound and lighting, wigs and makeup. Greg gives us the customary warning that they won't be a very responsive audience, as they will be taking notes of what they will need to do when we get to production week in the theatre and the technical rehearsal. This tends to be a feature of final runs: for instance Tim Mitchell the lighting designer will note where actors are standing so that he can have an idea as to how to sketch out the lighting plot for a particular scene; similarly Jeremy Dunn (sound) will note where any effects should go and if there are any special requirements such as radio-mikes. Wigs and costume will note any quick changes that may arise. Our final run is another step forward and left us poised in an excellent state of preparation for production week. We say au revoir to the rehearsal room with a glass of Cava and some nibbles bought, as with the end of *Dream* rehearsals, with Greg's Mobile Phone Fund.

However, I and several others have to limit our intake of sparkling wine as we have an evening understudy rehearsal – of the mad scene.

Saturday 19th July   THE official understudy line run in the afternoon and an evening show of *The Dream* ... there really is no rest for the wicked is there?

■

W E'VE had Sunday off and enter the theatre for our second technical rehearsal of the season. We are scheduled to tech for three full days, hopefully culminating in dress rehearsals on Wednesday night and Thursday afternoon before the first preview on Thursday evening. On entering the theatre for the first time it is clear that Rob Jones's model of the set that we saw seven weeks ago has been magnificently realised in situ as constructed by the Timothy's Bridge Road workshops. As planned it looks just like the *Midsummer Night's Dream* set, but the subtle differences do just as intended. The tall panels rotate to create entrances and exits, opening up the stage way back into the dark space behind the main acting area. A couple of semi-silvered panels become a two-way mirror for Claudius and Polonius to spy on Hamlet and Ophelia in the 'nunnery' scene.

Around the auditorium a scattering of cast and crew are taking in the new environment; there's the glow of computer screens, the murmur of muttered instructions into headsets, and the tap tapping of fingers on keyboards. The technology now available for theatre is amazing – digital sound, motorised lights and automatic flying all help to create the physical world of *Hamlet*. As for *The Dream* over three days each scene is painstakingly set up for light, sound, music and we slowly go through the play. The bulk of the time is spent on scene changes, any special effects that need to be tested and quick changes of costume that need to be practised and repeated as necessary.

Throughout the tech, as I did with Rod in *The Dream*, I make sure that I watch Patrick's scenes closely, making notes if necessary, so that I'm fully appraised

Monday 21st July to
Thursday 24th July

115

of any technical issues that come up for him and any re-blocking for the stage, just to keep ahead of the understudy game. I usually watch the first few previews on the monitor too, so that if called upon I have a visual memory of his performance.

We completed the tech in time to have a dress run on Wednesday evening. In the first dress we actors get back in the driving seat having not been in control for the best part of a week. That can be pretty tricky because there are so many new things to deal with, thus we tend to approach the event with caution rather than with all guns blazing to make sure we get through safely. It was a good dress run and we only stopped once when the players came on too early to set up for the play-within-a-play whilst we of the Danish court were still hanging some lanterns to light it, which was très amusant. Following the run, Greg decides that it'd be better to work on a couple of technically complex sequences on Thursday and forgo a second dress before our first preview, which is what we do in the lead up to playing in front of the paying public for the very first time.

I write this during our first preview, which is being attended by Gordon Brown and his entourage!

There's a bit of a shaky start for us on the battlements. You may recall that we decided that it'd be a great idea to enhance the creepiness of the first scene if the main sources of light were Marcellus and Barnado's torches. A development of this idea was that when the ghost was about to appear, our torches would flicker and go out under the influence of Old Hamlet's spectral ectoplasm. To enhance this effect the hi-tech solution to this was that the torches were to be radio-controlled by the LX department so that they would look as if they had a life of their own. Now it's the first preview: the audience is settling, Rob Curtis

starts his march around the stage as the lights dim and
Ewen bursts on to the stage barking out 'Who's there?'
blinding Rob with his light. We're off, so far so good.
On I come with Peter and we start the dialogue. Ewen
and I take turns to light whoever is speaking with
choreographic precision as worked out in rehearsal.
We didn't get very far when after about 30 seconds my
torch crashed out and could not be revived, so we were
left with Ewen's only to light the entire scene. However
our luminescent sorrows came not single spies when
about four minutes later Ewen's torch also went out,
leaving us to play a significant portion of the last
part of the scene in virtual darkness. How could this
happen, it worked fine in the tech? One theory is that
it could've been of the number of Special Branch radios
in and around the building interfering with our signal,
and true to say there are indeed many slightly scary
men in suits wandering around with radio thingies in
their ears. Whatever the cause, sometimes it's better to
play the simple ball, so to avoid a repeat it's decided that
we'll operate the lights manually with switches in the
traditional way from now on.

We've got to the interval and all is well, the audience
seem to be very much on our side and we're imbued
with the feverish excitement that goes with a first
preview.

We've just finished to a standing ovation; a truly
excellent show. Greg is very pleased and we're all
relieved to be up and running. Backstage afterwards
we're lined up to press the flesh with the Prime
Minister who was very jolly and charming as he was
when I met him a couple of years ago (just goes to show
that you shouldn't believe all you read in the papers),
then swiftly on to The Duck for an excited collective
debrief with drinks and chips and onion rings laid on,
which absolutely hits the post-show spot.

Sunday lovely Sunday

THE week of the technical and pressure of the first three previews was exciting but tiring. The show's in good shape so early on in its journey and developing in confidence with every performance in the lead up to press night. A little early extra drama last night though, we had our first understudy on. Ewen Cummins was poorly so David Ajala went on to play Barnado and was just great, especially given that the show is still settling in and he had to cope with the inevitable tweaks and changes made over these early performances. What with the busy week behind me Sunday is definitely going to be a day of rest.

Zoë has gone to visit her brother Simon with her mum in Cornwall and taken Milly the dog with her, so I'm home alone for the weekend. As such I intend to do nothing, or at least as little as possible. I ponder as to whether to buy and plant a plum tree – a long-promised project by me to Zoë – or go for a long bike ride. Being a Libran, I agonise over coffee and Sunday papers for some time. I haven't ridden my bike for ages so decide I'll do that as it's such a beautiful day, especially having spent most of the previous fortnight in the dark in a gigantic tin box ... on the other hand why not finally plant that plum tree? Oh dear, dither, dither, dither. But then, a stroke of genius ... I'll do both despite the day's declared rest status! I decide that first on the agenda is to get the plum tree and within seconds of my momentous decision, whip! I'm in the car and off to the Countrywide store near Bearley! The tree

purchased, and that at half-price in a clearance sale –
result! – it's back home and don't spare the 1300cc Ford
engine. It's a beautiful drive from Bearley to Alcester:
left off the main road along Salter's Way and under the
Edstone Aqueduct, at 754 feet the longest aqueduct
in England that carries the Stratford canal over the
railway line into Stratford and the disused trackbed of
the old Alcester to Bearley branch line. At this point
steam trains used to be able to replenish their water
tanks with canal water through a boxed pipe coming
down from the iron channel. Up and over the sharp
brow of Whitehouse Hill and one's stomach goes into
one's mouth as the plain sky of the upward climb tilts
away to yield to an intricate tapestry of Warwickshire
fields bounded by distant hills. Passing through Aston
Cantlow I resist the temptation of a pint at The King's
Head, a few more minutes and I'm home. Having been
inspired by the views of the countryside I resolve to go
for the ride first and *then* plant the tree.

My trusty bike has been cruelly abandoned outdoors
for some weeks in the garden and so needs some TLC.
The wheels and chain get a good oiling and the tyres
re-inflated. In fact it probably needs more than that
but I'm impatient to get on out there. After my hasty
cycle maintenance off I go on my trusty steed. Out
of Alcester, through Oversley Green and over the old
bridge, climbing up toward Oversley woods, over the
footbridge crossing the main Stratford to Alcester road,
then right and climb further up to the top of the hill
towards a farm marked out by two huge grain silos; a
landmark small and distant from the town but massive
and looming over me as I ride past them. Round
between two fields, the rapeseed harvested on my left
now green stubble, a golden field of wheat burning in
the summer sun to my right. In the distance there's the
growl of a tractor sowing seeds shrouded in a plume

of dust, and a host of birds trailing behind it in pursuit of lunch. Along a track toward the woods themselves then right, descending the hill towards Exhall, and the thrill of the effortless acceleration before the steep climb to Ardens Grafton. It's down through the gears and up through a place called Little Britain to the village itself. Past a carpenter's house with some beautiful hand-crafted birdhouses for sale in the garden, round to the left through the village; I stop to admire the magnificent view back across the valley. A gold and green patchwork of fields, the roofs of Exhall and the woods I'd just come from a blue-green strip. My destination now close by I coast along the gently sloping road to The Golden Cross. I park the bike in the garden and order a pint of local ale – Purity Gold brewed in Great Alne just up the road – then sit in the sun with the crossword for half an hour or so; bliss!

Suitably refreshed I'm back on the bike, up through the village to hurtle back down through Little Britain. Taking a slightly different route back – variety is the spice of and all that – I turn right at Exhall and off-road through a livery stable along a bridleway, past some horses then to open pasture. Past the stables to a gate at the edge of Oversley Woods the other side of which I pause while a combine harvester deposits grain into a hopper on the back of a tractor blocking the footpath. When it's finished I continue along the path round the back of the woods from Alcester, then under the A46 and onto the home stretch. Over and through more farmland and a field of maize, the rich green crop now head-high, having been barely knee-high only a few weeks ago. The path goes through a small paddock where two horses canter over to check me out having heard the clang of the gate as I open it. Their teeth noisily tear the grass that is their lunch. I wait for them to retreat, slightly anxious that if I ride straight past them they'll gallop after me … a fear that no doubt betrays the townie in me. The final stretch of path has become very overgrown, the going is slow, and at one point the long grass hides the path's steep camber. My bike goes from under me and I find myself staring at the cloudless sky cursing my carelessness. But no harm done, just a bruised elbow and knee, and I'm back in the saddle to emerge onto the old Stratford Road, back over the old bridge at Oversley Green and home.

After a much-needed glass of Hogan's cider, brewed in the neighbouring village of Haselor, it's time for my second major task of the day: the plum tree.

I proceed to dig a big hole in the garden, an activity I find surprisingly satisfying. As required it is dug to be twice as big as the pot I'd bought the tree in. In it goes, I pack the compost around it and stand back to admire my good work bedded in between the apple tree and the purple geraniums. I'm hot again and covered in mud so it must be time for another glass of cider.

My designated tasks complete I remember that the garden gate at the back has been sticking. It's been annoying me for some time so I set about digging up the stones in the path that've been causing the stick. Having dug them out I redistribute some of the sand and put the bricks back again. The gate has come unstuck but now I'm on a bit of a roll garden-wise, so I cut the grass and water all the plants. At last, all my work done, time for another refreshing glass of Hogan's finest, then I get under a cool shower to cleanse myself of mud and sand which by now I'm completely covered in. Feeling very smug, having already accomplished far more than intended, I just have Sunday dinner to cook. We have a great butcher in Alcester High Street and I bought a succulent piece of fillet steak as a bit of a treat on Saturday morning. I cook this rare and make a red wine and horseradish jus by deglazing the frying pan and serving it up with minted new potatoes and green vegetables. The steak beautifully tender melting like butter in the mouth, the piquant jus, astringent sweetness of the mint and potatoes and the fresh veg make for a DELICIOUS mains. For a simple pud, strawberries on lemon drizzle cake with sour cream. All this washed down with some fine red wine. It's now late evening, and the so-called day of rest had actually been pretty a satisfyingly active one, thus an early bed and a good night's sleep inexorably beckons before yet another busy week ahead and the second press night of the season.

A Pressing Engagement

Tuesday 5th August

IT'S press night at last. Having had the luxury of 10 previews the show is in very good nick. We've even started to get used to the hordes of people that flock to the stage door every night to see David or Patrick after the show; it really is like being in a rock band at the moment. Outside our dressing room window the excited chatter of fans grows steadily through the second half of the play as they arrive in dribs and drabs to wait patiently behind the barricades that have had to be erected to help control the throng. Soon after curtain down, as we in the Senior Common Room are getting changed, a huge cheer erupts and a supernova of flashbulbs glisters through the frosted glass windows as the Trekkies or Dr Who fans hail either or both of their heroes as they emerge from the stage door for pictures

and to sign some programmes. The RSC have taken the
precaution of hiring a private security firm to keep an
eye of things and most nights it's Big Dave (who judging
by appearances you *really* wouldn't mess with) keeping
an eye on things and escorting David to his car via a
secret exit so that he can get away with the minimum
of fuss. It must be very difficult for Patrick and David,
but especially David given the mega-interest in Dr Who
at the moment. It's very hard for him to simply come
for a post-show pint, after the first preview he had to
sneak over the garden wall at the back of The Duck and
keep a very low profile in the pub. Through rehearsals
at lunchtime he'd go out in the regulation disguise
of baseball cap and shades, which from what I could
see was surprisingly effective. However occasionally
he was spotted and asked to sign a card or book or
something, which he always did with great grace (he
really is a very nice chap). But of course he's not really
a time lord he's human. One lunchtime when he, me
and a couple of others were ordering baked potatoes in
one of the many take-away food shops in Stratford, a
lady who had ordered her food recognised him. She was
clearly delighted at this and started talking excitedly
at great length about how she wished her daughter
was there to meet him. David was very friendly and
chatted with her for a bit then turned to order his food,
but she wanted to continue the conversation. David
was impeccably polite if progressively briefer in his
responses as he, like all of us, only had an hour for
lunch and just wanted to get something to eat! There
was nothing particularly sinister or threatening about
the situation – the woman seemed perfectly nice – but
somehow a line had been crossed and David just had to
disconnect from her as politely as possible or he'd never
have got away.

Over the last week and a half of previews Greg has
tended to call us late in the afternoon for just a few
notes, which means that Cressida has managed to steal
extra time for understudy rehearsals. These have been
going really well, Claudius is finally cemented in my
brain – more or less – and we've been able to do some
detailed work on what makes him tick. A major feature
in his emotional landscape is his love for the queen.
Andrea Harris is understudying Gertrude and we've
done some great work together on their relationship
and what drives it. How much do they love each other?
Did they have an affair while old Hamlet was still alive?
How do they deal with the difficulty of their 'o'erhasty
marriage'? How do they cope with young Hamlet? And
what happens when things start to fall apart? We have
the understudy run on Monday 11th and we're all very
excited about it.

The other major work for me over the preview
period was getting up to speed on the sublime, funereal
Miserere. This has been tough but very satisfying, and
the hard work I've done on developing the particular
mode of my voice needed to perform the song has
extended my upper range by several notes. This means
that the sound I make has become less effortful and
hopefully more heavenly. The other thing is getting
used to singing in this unusual way in situ. One of
the purposes of the song is to cover the long slow
entrance of Ophelia's funeral procession through the
line of mirrors upstage of the grave, which are twisted
edgewise at 90 degrees to the auditorium to let us
through. The plan is that I follow the cortege and am
fitted with a radio mike so that I can start the song
offstage. But in the tech and dress I found that the
backstage jostle whilst Ophelia's corpse is lifted on
to the shoulders of the pallbearers and the mourners'
formation of an orderly queue interfered with my

preparation. I also had real trouble hearing the band.
It was decided that I come on from the opposite side
to the cortege, unseen in the dark at the back behind
the mirror line before they make their entrance. Then
on cue as the music starts they enter into a corridor
of light led by Jim as the priest and Zoë Thorne who
makes a completely convincing page boy. I get my first
note from the funeral bell and come in after a bar and a
half. We all know its one thing singing in the bath and
quite another singing in front of 1000 people. Well, in
the first couple of previews I tended to have a bit of a
wobble on the first note as even the slightest tension
adversely affected the accuracy of the crucial placing
of the voice; something I've never experienced before
singing in my normal 'chest' voice. In fact disaster
struck on the second preview. On I came as the bell
tolled, took my place up-centre, counted the bar and
a half of gently strummed D minor guitar chords, 1 ...
2 ... 3 ... 4 ... 1 ... 2... opened my mouth to sing and
out came what to my ears sounded like a cross between
a vulture and a pig-squeal. From absolutely nowhere
I'd somehow acquired the biggest frog-in-the-throat in
Christendom! OH GOD. The frog hopped away and I
got my voice back after a couple of agonising bars but
I was very embarrassed and apologised to Paul and to
Greg after who reassured me that it didn't sound as bad
as I'd thought. What I learned from THAT was that as
well as the pre-show warm up it's essential to warm up
my voice just before going on every night. Thankfully
to date no such horror has happened again. I can hear
the band better and come in with confidence. I was
quite daunted when my son Laurence and Shona, his
mum, came to see the show on the Thursday preview:
he's a fantastic musician and I was convinced he'd say I
was flat or out of time or something, but to my relief I
passed the filial acid test. I should add that he loved the

show – he's been studying *Hamlet* for A-levels and had been looking forward to seeing it very much.

Anyway, it's press day. In fact quite a few critics came yesterday on Monday, but this is the official day on which we declare ourselves up and running, all preparation done and, as far as is meaningful for something that is different every night, the finished article. We meet at four o'clock for a pep talk with Greg and some voice and text work with Lyn Darnley and Cis Berry. Greg reminds us that despite the presence of the press it is OUR Hamlet and not theirs, so we should forget they're there and just do what we normally do. 'Don't carry the baggage!' is his final note to us, by which he means: if something goes wrong forget it and move on – don't let it effect the whole evening. Lyn takes us through some vocal exercises on stage to get us to fill the space with sound. With Cis we each take a line from a section of a poem by Lorca ('Lament for Ignacio Sánchez Mejiás') and share it in various ways to get us speaking the text so that we can be heard but without pushing the volume; a balancing act of emphasising the consonants for clarity without sounding clipped and artificial. We stand in a circle, take a line each and read the whole poem round. This exercise is akin to a relay race where each runner takes the baton cleanly and passes it on without dropping it, keeping the words alive and full of energy. We do this several times until Cis is satisfied that we're doing the business and then she tells us to break up and recite the poem line by line whilst running around the entire auditorium. We each listen for our cue and when we speak our bit we have to jump in the air or stand on a seat or make an extravagant gesture to feed the energy of the language. In the final exercise we get as far away as we possibly can from each other on all levels of the theatre, from stage to gallery, and speak the poem as

quietly as we dare, whilst still being audible to the
person furthest away from us. Our final rehearsal call
done, united and ready for the rollercoaster ride ahead,
the company disperses, each actor now to spend the
remaining precious pre-performance time in their own
way.

Because of the huge amount of attention this
production has attracted there is a particularly excited
atmosphere pervading the theatre and a feeling of great
anticipation. The table in the dressing room corridor is
groaning with champagne bottles and flowers and once
again the customary exchange of cards and gifts takes
place. This time we each get a personalised bottle of
champagne from David (very lovely, very generous), a
personalised rap-poem from Ricky Champ written in
felt pen on blue shiny card, Danish pastries from John
Woodvine, bottles of beer from Patrick (very Danish,
very Claudian). In addition there is a salad of flowers,
chocolates and sweeties to enjoy.

The inexorable countdown continues with the
compulsory pre-performance calls, a flying call for the
aerial work, the fight call and a song call for me. It is
now The Half (35 minutes before curtain-up) and we
start to get into costume. Everyone is in high spirits
and the dressing room banter flows freely with its usual
good-natured ruthlessness. Suddenly Greg bursts in to
take a breather from the hurly-burly of the press-night
crowd, TV crews and general noise to wish us good luck
once again. Beginners' is called and Ewen and I troop
along the corridor, through the old Michel Saint-Denis
rehearsal room (now the main backstage area where
the crew sit and where we pick up our props, do quick
changes etc) and into the wings where we hear the
buzz of the full house live. We wait until final clearance
from front of house, and when that's given Suzi hands
over control via her radio to Klare our Deputy Stage

Manager way up in the glass box at the back of the gallery.

We're off! Rob Curtis enters as Francisco with the house lights up, the audience hush, the house lights dim. Ewen, Peter and I are ushered through the pass door by Katie our Assistant Stage Manager and we creep to our starting positions behind the audience. All the lights snap out, Ewen's torch snaps on and once again the first line cracks through the darkness like a starting pistol … 'Who's there?'

The next three-and-a-half hours fly by and we've done it. The audience have been very responsive and applaud enthusiastically at the end. Press night audiences are usually atypical and include a combination of critics making notes, loved ones worrying that things go well and people in the business who've come along for the occasion. This tends to result in HUGE reactions to the show coming from one part of the auditorium and hardly anything from another. Anyway, what's done is done so back to Dressing Room D for some celebratory glasses of bubbly while we get into our glad rags for the party. I'm going to meet Zoë and Janet there, who've been watching. People do the rounds backstage with their congratulations. My agent (Sarah Barnfield of Price Gardner who also represents one of my dressing room buddies Rod Smith) has come up from London with a casting director (Louise Cross), so I emerge as quickly as I can to say hello. She's as supportive as ever and Louise is very complimentary – fingers crossed for some TV work when I'm free next February. After a short chat they're off on the motorway to get back to London. Finally I leave the theatre to the hotel where the party is and it's RAMMED full; almost immediately I give up any hope of locating Zoë. After about an hour enough people have left so that the venue isn't quite so suffocating but

I still haven't found Z and am enticed on to the dance floor where – aided by two large glasses of red wine and a beer on top of the dressing-room champagne and therefore perhaps a little *too* enthusiastically – I throw some shapes ... well what the hell, its press night! Finally I locate Zoë in the garden where I've gone to cool down and we catch up. Naturally she thinks I'm marvellous, and loves the production too. She leaves a little later to take her mum home, but I stay for more excited chatter and another beer and swipe me it's 2:00 a.m. and the bar is closing. This can only mean one thing: back to The Ferry House for a nightcap. This RSC residence comprises several bedsits and is a common refuge for those whose press night is not quite complete. Back there it's one more glass of wine and a few more laughs until finally fatigue wins over excitement. After a taxi ride home I'm greeted by Milly the dog who is sleepy and mystified by my tardy arrival, her silhouette looming over me at the top of the stairs like The Hound of the Baskervilles, and I finally hit the hay at about 4:30, just before 'the dawn in russet mantle clad walks o'er the dew of yon high eastward hill' ... zzzzzzzzzzzzzzzz ...

A COMPLETE write-off and fortunately I'm not called for any understudy rehearsals. I finally surface about midday with a SCREAMING hangover and spend most of the day horizontal on the sofa repeating that mantra well-known to all who've supped too much of the grain or grape or both... 'Never again!' ... Yeah right!

Wednesday 6th August

Thursday 7th August

AFTER press night, and a personal detox, today is the only chance for the understudy company to work through the whole play before the understudy technical tomorrow, and thank goodness Cressida has managed to steal the time she did at the latter end of the principal rehearsals for *Hamlet*. I've loved working with her and she's done a great directing job on the understudy production.

Friday 8th August

A SMALL call in the morning then we start the tech in the afternoon. There's a tighter than usual timetable on this one as *Love's Labour's Lost* starts rehearsal next Tuesday, so we'll need to finish the tech by Monday morning in order to have a run that afternoon. I really hope we can: not only from the purely professional point of view of wanting to play Claudius from start to finish in real time as close to performance conditions as possible, but equally because I think we've all done some fantastic work and it'd be a shame not to have the opportunity to play our version together at least once.

The afternoon goes well and we're on schedule. The significant technical challenges for me are that there are quite a few costume and wig changes for Claudius/ Ghost – no nightmare ones though some of them pretty swift – but I was well looked after by Yvonne Gilbert (Patrick's dresser) and Rachel Seal and Kimberley Boyce (wig girls extraordinaire).

At 5:00 we break for a meeting with Greg. We'd all wondered what this was about and it seems that Illuminations Media are interested in producing a live broadcast of *Hamlet* to be shown in cinemas around the UK the Sunday after our season is due to finish (so *that's* what that lunchtime meeting was about back in April!). Apparently this is something the Metropolitan Opera in New York have done with great success and seems like a brilliant idea, especially given the number of people who won't have been able to get tickets to see the show at The Courtyard. We've all got to agree to it and as far as the filthy lucre goes everyone involved will be paid the same ... it gets better and better, what's not to like?

W E made it! The tech finished in time, the actual run was great fun and all and sundry acquitted themselves with great applomb. The feedback from those who saw it was excellent, and given the mighty colossus that is the actual role of Hamlet special mention must go to Ed Bennett who was brilliant. There was a worrying moment when Ed fell off stage in the closet scene – he really hurt his leg and it was touch and go as to whether he'd go on in the evening. Anyway, it was with excited relief that we all tucked into our tea and buns in the green room afterwards. It's a funny thing though, having worked so closely and intensely, particularly with Andrea, Ed and Rod as Polonius, that if any of us have to step into the breech it won't be with our co-understudies but our principals. In that respect the understudy run is a special one-off experience to be treasured – although we're hoping to do it again in London.

Monday 11th August

Love's Labour's Last

Tuesday 12th August

WITH no time to draw breath following yesterday's understudy exertions and subsequent celebratory drinks after last night's evening show, today we of Blue Company start work on the final play of our part of the season, *Love's Labour's Lost*, and we welcome a final friend into the fold – Nina Sosanya will play Rosaline, the feisty foil to Berowne's mordant mirth. Nina is a lovely actress and although we didn't work together we were in the company at the same time in 2003 when she gave a fine Rosalind in *As You Like It*.

The now familiar first-day ritual gets underway. A rallying chat from Greg, a peep at the costume design and model of the set, then slowly start to work through the play. Francis O'Connor's design is beautiful and quite a contrast both to the coldness of Elsinore and the elision of 20th century Athens with the gambolling fairy fantasy world in the *Dream*. This time we are firmly in the Elizabethan era. The cozzies are sumptuous and the environment yet another fresh spin on the *Dream/Hamlet* set. We have the tall mirrors fixed slightly further back than for the other shows, creating two extra entrances either side upstage. The main difference is arboreal in nature ... a whacking great tree thrusts up through the black slabs of the paved floor, its giant tentacle-like roots clawing their way across the stage. Apparently the tree is climbable, which particularly excites Ricky Champ who's playing Costard the clown.

REMARKABLY we managed to get through the sitting-down-and-putting-it-into-our-own-words stage of rehearsals in just four days … *Hamlet* took two weeks! I love *Love's Labour's Lost*, I wish it was done more often, but it is pretty tricky. *Hamlet* is a deep and complex dissection of themes most of us can relate to in some way – love, death, alienation, betrayal, powerlessness etc. In a way *Love's Labour's* is the opposite, a pastoral comedy of manners; simpler philosophically but the context far removed from our 21st-century sensibilities, being firmly rooted in the Elizabethan court. There are a lot of obscure contemporary references to unpick, and Elizabethan jokes that we must make funny; I sense that with this one the sooner we get on our feet and start playing around the better. My workload for *LLL* is very light – I play Marcade who doesn't turn up until near the very end. In addition I'm understudying Dull, which is just fine: not too much extra pressure to maintain in addition to Peter Quince and of course Claudius.

Alongside *Hamlet*'s opening and the early days of *LLL*, The Captain Of Our Fairy Band rehearsals continue. We've quite a set building up now and need to start polishing the songs and getting them to performance standard. We're hoping to play at the *Love's Labour's* first night party and maybe a gig in The Dirty Duck at some point. A major addition to our musical armoury is Sam Dutton who has brought his violin up from London, and Ed's dead keen to bring his guitar to the party.

Absolutely wonderful news on Thursday – Laurence got his A-level grades so is off to Oxford in October!

Sunday 17th August

TODAY we went *en famille* to Ragley Hall Country Fair. We'd never been before, and the slightly dodgy weather held up so we spent a good few hours there. I had a go at the archery, watched some falconry, and simply had to sample some local real ale. Milly was in dog heaven – people! other dogs! food! smells! She was a little disturbed by horses en masse; she's seen them on walks in the country but not so many in full galloping glory in the display area. I went round Ragley Hall itself which is very interesting not least because the family tree of the owner, the Marquess of Hertford, criss-crosses some of those aristocratic families Shakespeare wrote about: Edward III; The Plantagenets; Harry 'Hotspur' Percy; leading on to Jane Seymour, Henry VIII's third wife and therefore, I suppose, Elizabeth I's step-mum for a brief moment. The view from the front steps of the house looking out over the fields to Oversley Wood is wonderful, and is the reverse perspective to the one I'm used to. Normally on the regular dog walk around the side of Oversley I'm looking back over the fields to the Palladian splendour of the house and the very spot I was standing on.

Monday 18th August

WE did *The Dream* for the first time in a month this evening. When there's a gap of 10 days or more in the run of a production we have to do a line run. This entails all the cast who speak sitting in a circle and simply bashing through all the lines of the play as quickly as possible thus brushing the cobwebs from our collective synapses that store the words and moves for the show. We also had a song call to refresh our memories music-wise. It was a pleasure to return to our faithful Athenian friend and we slid easily back into the saddle.

T HROUGH the week work has continued on *Love's Labour's*. I wasn't called until this afternoon for my bit although there were a couple of music rehearsals for the songs at the very end of the play. We've also been given research projects on various things germane to the play that'll help us understand its contemporary significance more fully. Subjects range from the real King of Navarre, to hunting, to owls, to schoolmasters, to the socialites of the day. My project is Arcadia: I wanted to do this as the name of my character is a play on words meaning to spoil paradise, i.e. mar-arcady. *LLL* is a pastoral comedy so my task is to try to find any connections between the pastoral idyll that was the Arcadia of myth and Shakespeare's play.

I'm also doing some stuff for Open Day on the 31st August. Open Day is an annual event when the RSC throw open their doors and let the public see what happens behind the scenes, as well as concerts, talks and events. I'm singing and reading in a concert of past RSC music in the church, and also taking part in a poetry session the theme of which is gardens. Oh yes, and a reading of *Fratricide Punished* which is a bizarre version of Hamlet. Cressida has dug up this 1920s English translation of an 18th-century German translation of an older play that *might* be some of the source material for Shakespeare's Hamlet ... erm, I

Friday 22nd August

hope that's clear. Under Cressida's direction some of us – basically the understudy company – prepared and read it to the others during *Hamlet* rehearsals. Greg thought that we should do it for Open Day and so we are, in the evening I think.

Sunday 24th August

WHILST next Sunday certainly won't be a day of rest today certainly is. Peter and his other half Sarah have thrown a barbecue at her parents' house. Everyone is very relaxed and al fresco and i'm glad at the opportunity for them to meet Zoë properly. The weather is kind to us and our lovely hosts have prepared some very tasty food. It's a great party!

Bottoms up!

Monday 25th August
to Thursday
28th August

HAVING done a first work-through of the play last week we go back to the beginning again and, as I appear right at the end, once again it's a very light week for me. I feel quite ambivalent about this: on the one hand I have some free time so that I can keep up with my own interests, practising my bass and the songs for The Captain Of Our Fairy Band, and my guitar for myself; on the other as I've said I love the play and wish I was more involved in it.

That said I have a voice call with Lyn on Tuesday and come in for some research project work, and on Wednesday in the evening we have a flamenco session, which I LOVE, not least because of my interest in guitar music and techniques of all kinds. The posture of the flamenco dance is very held and upright, very formal but erotically charged and Greg wants us to use this to explore the physicality of the characters and the undercurrent of sensuality between The King of Navarre (Ed Bennett) and his courtiers – Longaville (Tom Davey), Dumain (Sam Dutton) and Berowne (David Tennant) – and The Princess of France (Minnie Gale) and hers – Katherine (Kathryn Drysdale), Maria (Natalie Walter) and Rosaline (Nina Sosanya). I'm awestruck at the guitar playing of the accompanist and it's great to let off all my surplus energy with a bit of a dance.

■

YOU may recall that way way back in this little book I explained the complexity of the understudy 'knock-on' effect. Namely that if an actor is off and his/her understudy has to go on this means that the understudy's understudy goes on etc etc. I somewhat nerdily likened it to the so-called 'Butterfly Effect' in chaos theory in that, according to the theory, just as the flutter of a butterfly's wing in one continent can cause a hurricane on the other side of the world if, for instance, a mechanical is off in Athens there's chaos in fairyland. Well tonight just that has happened! Unfortunately Joe is off as Bottom so Ricky is on in his stead. This means that Rob Curtis has to cover Snout the Tinker for him and Peter De Jersey plays Theseus for Rob whilst retaining Oberon, meaning that those nightmarish, lightning quick changes teched back in May have become reality. Rob also has various duties as a fairy, those of which he can't fulfil we'll pick up as we go.

The first hint that something was amiss was in the greenroom at the rehearsal rooms in the morning. Most of us were having a cuppa just before a full company call for the presentation of our *Love's Labour's Lost* research projects, bantering away cheerfully as usual, when Suzi entered and said, 'Ricky I need to talk to you' in such a way that silenced the room. 'Oh … right' said Ricky, he smiled, shrugged and followed her out. Looks were exchanged, eyebrows raised but in a second the bubble of silent puzzlement burst and the chatter resumed. Then a couple of times during the project presentations Greg alluded somewhat cryptically to the fact that Ricky was 'busy'. I assumed that he had an extra class with Majella Hurley, our dialect coach; he's playing Costard and the accent they're going for is rural Essex, which is quite unusual. It was only after lunch that the position became clear: Joe was indisposed, Ricky was to play Bottom that night, and so he was rehearsing with Cressida at The Courtyard. Now, although David Ajala had gone on for Ewen Cummins a few weeks ago as the understudy pioneer of the Blue season, boldly going where none of us hitherto had gone before, the mechanics of his heroic moment were relatively easy. The consequences for this substitution were more far-reaching.

Greg proposed that we truncate rehearsals for the afternoon so that people could be free to join Ricky, Peter and Rob to rehearse for the evening's show on stage at the theatre. Cressida had prioritised the mechanicals' scenes and the play scene for Ricky as Bottom, Rob as Snout and Peter as Theseus. Then Peter and Rian Steele (Hippolyta) had a fight call and went through their other two scenes, with me helping out as Egeus. A bit of a break for food and for people to gather their wits, then just before the half we had a flying call so that I could practise getting Ricky into his harness, which Rob normally does. Then it was countdown to curtain up hoping that we hadn't missed something.

If ever one ever wanted an example of ensemble actors working together it is in a situation such as this. Things got off to a cracking start with Peter in the first scene. Rob watched on the monitor in the wings and found it quite a surreal experience, not least because the tyranny of logistics meant that he'd had to give up his bigger principal role (Theseus) to play his smaller understudy role … such is the cruel nature of the knock-on sometimes. As I changed out of Egeus's formal suit into the black, heavy cotton, goat-legged, all-in-one body suit, biker boots and fishnet stocking mask that comprise my fairy costume, I heard the first mechanicals scene on the tannoy, the audience audibly having a rip-roaring time as usual, Ricky out of the blocks to a great start. I was fascinated by his variations on Bottom's theme, different to Joe but still maintaining the integrity of the production; but that's how extraordinary these plays are, deep vessels into which the individual actor pours his personality, the text-defined shape taken is the same but the flavour of the contents unique.

As we fairies go on with Hermia and Lysander, I whisper to Sam Dutton to go upstage of the couple in order to take up his position standing in for Rob; he's the log that Hermia rests her head on stage right that mirrors me as the stage-left log. After the scene with Helena and Demetrius and then Hermia's awakening to find Lysander gone, it's the mechanicals' rehearsal scene in the forest. Again everything goes smoothly, Bottom appears in his ass's head and we fairies chase the rest off as monsters made out their own tools. Then the fairy band crawl under the stage to be summoned by Andrea as Titania, up through the traps with the doll puppets to do her bidding, she having fallen in love with a new ass. Katie has wrapped the loop that Rob normally has charge of for me to hitch to the karabiner on Bottom's flying rope round my doll so that I cannot possibly forget it, which would be ghastly (Katie is a real gem). We crouch under the stage until our cue comes to emerge from the floor of the forest, and I'm petrified that I'll drop the loop back down the trap – which would be equally ghastly – so I put it round my neck for safe keeping. Up we come for our first close-up interchange with Bottom in the play and clearly Ricky is having a ball. I take extra care to thread the loop through all three loops on the harness, double-check they're secure, Sam Alexander clips him in and up he goes! End of part one.

The second half starts as normal with the big lovers' scene, and then they are led 'up and down' in confusion by Puck and the rest of us fairy-folk. Rob is back as a fairy for this as he does a fair bit of lifting and physical stuff. After 'up and down', off I go to get changed back into Egeus. On my way back to the stage for the lovers awakening there are a number of dressers and wardrobe people poised for the impossibly quick change Peter has to do to go from Oberon to Theseus both of which are quite complicated costumes; there are actually no lines of text to cover for this, so the music cue for the scene change has been extended. His riding boots open, tunic and trousers laid out ready for his imminent arrival, like a pit stop in a Formula 1 motor race. The scene finishes, dressers are coiled ready to spring into action as we see Peter make his exit on the backstage monitor. He bursts through the double doors that lead from the wings to the backstage area and OFF comes the Oberon costume in triple-quick time and ON goes Theseus in quadruple-quick time – I count 40 seconds and the complete costume change is achieved. Out of the metaphorical pits, on he runs following Hyppolyta to find the lovers asleep. Egeus leaves the story after this scene, a shamed and lonely figure, so I've only got the company song at the end. Before that though, I can hear the final play scene go down a storm as I wait in the dressing room. Rob goes great guns and gets all his laughs as Wall in the play and Ricky is on fire as Bottom. Peter has one more express change from Theseus to Oberon, and we're home and dry. At the curtain call Ricky takes the last solo bow as Bottom and gets well-earned cheers from the audience and applause from us for a job well done; he later says that it was the most exciting night he's ever had on stage and I know what he means.

A *DREAM* matinee and Joe is back so order is restored and a normal show except …

It happened near the end when the lovers wake up having been restored to their proper partners by Puck. The Athenian court enters from the wedding-morning hunt led by Hyppolyta, who outruns Theseus into this beautifully romantic scene, there is some sumptuous, emotionally-charged music from Paul Englishby, and wonderfully warm lighting to suggest dawn and the start of a new day, a new beginning. The lovers, discovered by the Duke and his retinue, struggle sleepily to their feet, vulnerable and childlike – a delicate moment. Then as Tom Davey drew breath to speak, I was aware of a bit of a kerfuffle stage left. A lady in a bright floral dress in the front row had got up from her seat and with her back to the stage was desperately edging past her fellow audience members in order to make a speedy exit. Suddenly an unmistakeable noise rattled out like a machine gun, strafing the stage and reverberating around the entire Courtyard … it was possibly one of the biggest farts I'd ever heard. Tom froze for a nanosecond and started his speech slowly and carefully with the telltale crazed eyes and quivering gargoyle-like grimace of a mouth that betrays an actor on the edge of hysterical laughter. I looked round at my other colleagues and could see that they were all in a similar straits, indeed I could feel a laughter start to balloon in my belly and make its way to my throat and must assume that I too had the same rictus expression on my face. What's more I was next to speak and of course Egeus is not a character renowned for jollity so I had to be extra-angry to stem the tide of cachinnation rising within me. God knows how but we all made it through the scene without dissolving into a mass corpse, although no-one dared look anyone else in the eyes, until we all collapsed in tears safely out of earshot backstage; oh the deep joy of live theatre – Bottom, quite literally, causes chaos again! Which only goes to show … a little broken wind from the stalls can cause a hurricane of hilarity onstage.

Open Day

A S I've mentioned today is Open Day, a festival-like event when the RSC throws open its doors to the public giving them an opportunity to get some idea of the behind-the-scenes work that goes on, join in workshops, enjoy concerts, football matches and the like. So it was an earlier than usual Sunday wake-up time for me, and worse for poor Zoë as she was stage managing the first events at The Courtyard, the flying demo and rope-work etc, and had to be in at 8:00 ... needless to say, to avoid the rustle of divorce papers I didn't moan to her about my 10:30 start. Anyway, in the car and off I went to start the day on time. On arrival, having first collected my packed lunch and Open Day T-shirt (first things first), my first engagement of the day was a photo shoot. Members of the company had been asked to be in a group photograph to go to the press that Monday to launch an appeal to raise £1m for the redevelopment fund.

I make my way round to the riverside of the theatre behind The Swan where the artists' block is to be built to accommodate dressing rooms, the greenroom etc, and join my colleagues. Ellie Kurttz (who also took our fab production and rehearsal photos) arranged the grouping. Some of us draped over the scaffolding cladding the back of the building, others perched on a stepladder all framing a huge card showing the Theatres Appeal logo, held up by our press officer Nada Zakula squashed precariously out of sight behind it at the top of the ladder. Michael Boyd, Vikki Heyward (the Executive Director) and Greg, John Woodvine, Patrick, and David complete the frame sitting in front and below it. I had one eye on my watch as Alison Bomber had rung to say that there was a last-minute rehearsal for the choir and orchestra at the Holy Trinity Parish Centre in preparation for a lunchtime concert of RSC music in the Church. There is a huge collection of scores for shows going back over 100 years that have languished in the archive unperformed for decades – wonderful stuff, some of which John Woolf and Greg have excavated for this concert. I arrived, hot and scant of breath having legged it the full length of Southern Lane, and was delighted to see Forbes Masson again. He's a fabulous singer and actor and was in the legendary *Histories*, and we were booked to read an excerpt from *Richard II* together backed by incidental music written by a then unknown Vaughan Williams for the Shakespeare Memorial Theatre in 1908. We were also to sing a duet as Oberon and Puck, a setting of their dialogue following Titania's falling in love with Bottom as an ass, written by Richard Peaslee for Peter Brook's iconic *Dream* in 1971. In true Open Day flying-by-the-seat-of-your-pants spirit this rehearsal was actually the first occasion that all – nay not all … *most* – of the musicians, singers and readers for the concert were all in the same room together at the same time. With about half an hour to go we crossed the road to Shakespeare's church itself to practise whatever we could before the public were let in at one o'clock. The concert went brilliantly, it was fascinating to hear these hidden treasures hitherto unheard for such a long time. The audience were very appreciative and I hope more of these jewels are dusted off and polished in the future. After the concert there was no time to draw breath for me as it was straight into the poetry reading which followed hard upon. Its theme was gardens, the programme put together by Lyn Darnley. For this, we really had NO time to rehearse, and the public were let in as we were setting up. But onward and upward, it was a triumph and the church was a wonderfully atmospheric venue to read in, if a little tricky acoustically for the spoken word. Its funny how an element of busk gives a performance an edge that more often than not works for the good: Open Day demonstrates this par excellence.

My duties done for the morning I wandered over to the theatre gardens to have a look at the football. It was the middle of a match between Mace, the building contractors and sponsors of Open Day, and a team of my fellow actors. I watched for a bit, cheering on my colleagues. It looked like great fun, played in good humour, with the ball ending up in The Avon more than once to be rescued by passing boaters. Unfortunately the actors lost, the main blame in post-match analysis being laid to footwear; whilst they had slithered around on the increasingly muddy grass in their trainers, the Mace team had been well equipped with proper boots. As I was leaving, another team of actors were preparing to play the staff from The Dirty Duck; apparently they lost that one too, a goal of theirs that would've given them a draw having been somewhat controversially disallowed. I made my way through the crowds to the car; there was a real buzz all along the waterside and a great turnout for the day despite the slightly inclement weather.

Back in the car I set off for Bearley. I'd arranged to have lunch at Zoë's mum's as her aunt Beezie, cousin Jeremy and his wife Dee and three-year-old daughter Alice were visiting. It was great to see them again – Dee is expecting twins so there's a lot of excitement about that. They'd been in Stratford in the morning; apparently Alice particularly liked the 'Dressing Up Box' costume workshop, the sonnet readings on the ferry across the river and the tour of the RST building site. What a renaissance girl she is!

Having had a delicious lunch, a natter and a bit of
a sit down with the Sunday papers I was back in the
car to Stratford for the evening to give my Claudius
– or rather, Erico – in the staged reading of *Fratricide
Punished*. The script we used was based on William
Poel's prompt copy for the performances at the Oxford
Playhouse in August 1924 and in October of that year
at the New Oxford and Little Theatres in London. It's
difficult to know how funny Mr Poel intended the script
to be but our audience laughed uproariously just as,
according to contemporary accounts, they did in 1924.
We were finished by 9:30, and it was into party clothes
for a fundraising do at The Duck for two charities being
supported by Kev Wimperis and Matt Aston (both are
members of The Courtyard stage crew) – Children With
Leukaemia and Cancer Research UK respectively. To
raise money they're both in training for the New York
marathon. It was very jolly and after a well-earned pint,
tired but happy, I made my way home.

Teeming autumn big with rich increase ...

Labouring On

TODAY everyone is delighted that Ewen Cummins is unable to make tonight's performance of *Hamlet* and has to make way for his understudy David Ajala! Why is this? Are the cracks starting to appear in the company's camaraderie? Is the ensemble fragmenting and a corrosive enmity creeping in? What evil deed has Ewen done to deserve our glee at his indisposal? Or is he simply THAT BAD as Barnado? Well … he became a daddy for the second time!!! His partner Dids gave birth to a little girl yesterday so he's taking time off to tend to this beautiful little addition to his family; thus the reason to celebrate his absence.

LOVE'S *Labour's* has been a strange show for me as I haven't been in rehearsals very much at all. However this week my involvement in the show has increased in that, to help create a sense of the wider community of Navarre, there will be an interval interlude of Navarrian villagers singing rounds and dancing. We've started work on these with Bruce O'Neil, the Musical Director for *LLL*, and Mike 'Movement' Ashcroft. Some of the songs are contemporary with Shakespeare, some a little later; appropriately enough they tell of love lost and won and of country life and some of them are very rude! We've been getting to grips with how to weave the songs and dances into a narrative and how we might achieve this practically. In fine weather we'll start outside The Courtyard, move into the foyer and then into the

theatre itself. If it's rainy we'll need to be flexible as
the foyer'll be very crowded ... hmmm ... we probably
won't know how it'll work until we do it in public, but if
we get it right it should be a lot of fun.

Today I had a costume fitting for Marcade, the
French nobleman who has travelled to Navarre to
interrupt the revels of the young to tell the Princess of
her father's death. The Princess hints that her father is
ill near the very beginning of the play, but no further
mention is made until Marcade arrives after a scene
where the four sets of lovers deride the country folks'
performance of *The Nine Worthies* and then bait Don
Armado. The action at this point is cruelly comedic and
the arrival of the angel of death completely unexpected;
a remarkable moment when the mood of the play
transforms and the young realise that its time to grow
up. My costume is being especially made for me and
at this stage is half finished, which meant that I was
in tailor's dummy mode while the merits of different
fabrics, ruff sizes etc were compared and discussed and
different patterns chalked or pinned about my person.
It'll look amazing, and whilst I think that Shakespeare
works perfectly well in modern dress if the aesthetic is
carefully conceived, I do love wearing period clothes:
they can be very powerful to wear and ignite the
imagination.

S OME unwelcome excitement and a terrible sense
of déjà vu as the rain poured and poured over
Warwickshire. Last year we were badly flooded and out
of our new home for over six months, and our hearts
were in our mouths that this might happen again as the

Saturday
September 6th

Arrow and Alne rivers were put on flood watch; they join about 100 metres from our house.

In the morning I was called for a guitar session with Nick Lee who's in the RSC band. There's a scene in the play when the Prince and his chums catch each other out, overhearing the love poems each has written to the object of his affection, despite the fact that they've all sworn to forswear love. It's been decided that Sam Alexander will sing his poem as Dumain. The four-footed tetrameter of Dumain's poem lends itself to being sung, so Paul has set it to music and Sam will accompany himself on the ukulele (his playing has really come on not least because of band rehearsals!). David Ajala is his understudy and he can't play the ukulele or guitar; it's mooted that if he goes on I'll accompany him, so I'll need to learn the music to Sam's song. It's a very enjoyable session even if I do have a weather eye on the weather.

I spent my moments offstage in the *Hamlet* Saturday matinee checking the Environment Agency website for developments, and while onstage I struggled to put the thought of our lovely house being overwhelmed by cold murky floodwaters AGAIN to the back of my mind. I didn't have an evening show so went straight home after the matinee. The Arrow was swollen and running fast full-brim to its banks. Through the afternoon Zoë, like me, had been glued to the news and praying for the rain to stop. Our confidence in the situation wasn't helped by the fact that it has been publicly acknowledged for some time that Alcester needs three new pumping stations – the process for their installation is bewilderingly slow. The evening passed, Zoë cooked a cottage pie, and in escapist-mode we watched Saturday telly, ate food, drank wine and crossed our fingers ...

■

IT'S morning and the crisis is over. We're in the clear and very relieved, and thinking of the poor souls who'd become victims this time round.

■

THE good news is that LLL took several strides forward last week, the bad news is that the simul-broadcast of *Hamlet* collaboration between Illuminations Media and the RSC that was being planned and put together for the Sunday 16th November had to be cancelled. It was an immensely complex thing to arrange and unfortunately it seems that there simply wasn't enough time to draw all the necessary strings together.

Anyway, life goes on and today Patrick threw a big garden party at his house for the whole company on what turned out to be a beautiful, golden, early autumn sunny day. Once again he was a kind and generous host – superb food, great wine – and it was wonderful for us all to get out of Stratford and chill out together in such tranquil surroundings. It was also an opportunity for The Captain Of Our Fairy Band to play its first gig. We set up outside the French windows overlooking Patrick's garden and played a handful of songs from our set in the open air to our mates, which was great fun, and who knows perhaps next year Glastonbury beckons … meanwhile we definitely plan to do a gig in Stratford before we leave.

Friday 19th
September

REHEARSALS over the last two weeks or so have followed the rhythm of the first two plays – working through the play in increasing detail, adding some things, cutting others and then sometimes reinstating them. Cress has once again managed to squeeze in some understudy rehearsals and I've had the odd voice and dialect call with Majella to perfect my rural Essex for my Dull understudy. Today we had our first run and we have a very good launch pad from which to dive into our final week's rehearsal.

Whilst I've not been called much for the main rehearsals I've been very involved in the songs and the dances, which are going to be great. We've decided which songs we're going to sing in the interval and the full company have also worked a lot on Paul's four-part setting for the 'Owl and the Cuckoo' song at the very end of the play. As has become usual for me at the RSC, given the fact that the men in the company far outnumber the women, I've been drafted in to sing the alto line, which is great as it'll also help to keep my upper voice in trim for the song in *Hamlet*. Mike's choreographed a kind of cross between a morris and a clog dance for the country dancing, set to a raunchy, folky arrangement. It's noisy and earthy and brilliant. I think the plan is that after singing the rounds outside and in the foyer, we lead the audience in and dance the dance on stage to open the second half of the evening.

Also over the last couple of weeks, subsequent to the arrival of 'Peanut' as Ewen's new baby was initially dubbed (by him I hasten to add!), he has for obvious reasons suffered a fair bit of sleep deprivation, so has built a sort of nest in the dressing room. He has put a mattress under his counter and draped a couple of

calico gowns from wardrobe to block out the rest of us
so he can cat-nap to make up for his nocturnal slumber
deficit. The normal function of these garments is to
protect one's costume backstage, especially where
there's food and drink involved – they're de rigeur in
the green room at tea-time – but now they have a new
purpose. We of the Senior Common Room have dubbed
Ewen's nest 'Sleepy Hollow'. Another consequence of
this is that I have extra duties as his co-member of the
Danish security services in Hamlet. We do nearly all
our scenes together, and I am thus charged with being
his alarm clock while he gets his 40 winks whenever
he can during the performance, waking him up when
his services are required onstage. I have to say that
depending on how deep he is in the Land of Nod, this
can often take more than one attempt.

O VER the last week we've put into practise what
we've learned from the first run and worked
hard to move forward from that. Each successive
run, last Wednesday and the final run today, was an
improvement on the one before as confidence with the
complex and often obscure language grew.

Friday 26th
September

Much earlier in rehearsal Cis Berry had said that the
humour and wit of the play lies not only in the precise
meanings of the language but in its raw sounds and
rhythms. For the last run it crackled along and I think
we've got a very witty, elegant show on our hands. I
can't wait for us to put it in front of an audience for the
first time.

Sunday
28th September

WALKING the dog earlier today, the harvested fields lay brown beneath a milky autumn sky, and the leaves were starting to turn their colour and fall, thus confirming that summer is over. I felt a slight melancholy to think that our season here only has a few weeks to run before we go to London for the winter. Inevitably my thoughts turned to next year's big ensemble project, which of course I'd love to be part of, as I know quite a few of us do, and I'm sure there'll be a lot of competition to get in on it. I plotted my triumphant return as Milly snuffled around the edge of the woods and scampered along the path without a care in the world. How nice it must be to be a dog and have no concept of the future, to enjoy the moment and be concerned simply with doggy things – smells, food, chasing rabbits and birds – with no need to worry about work, careers or money.

Another Opening, another show

Monday
29th September

IT'S the first day of the *Love's Labour's* technical rehearsal already.

We had a song call for 'The Owl and the Cuckoo' at 12:00 then looked at part of the interval show on stage around lunchtime. Francis's set is stunning, and the final variation on the overall scenic theme of the season has absolutely worked a treat. Having grown from a

mere sapling in the model to full size, the huge tree
is really HUGE, its canopy casting leafy shadows over
the playing area, and the thick roots clawing their way
toward the audience across the width of the stage.

I was only called for an hour and then went home.
In the unlikely event that we get to the end of the play
today, Suzi B will give me a ring.

I N my absence yesterday they'd got as far as the
interval so I'm called very first thing to get into
make-up and wigs to tech the interval sequence proper.

Tuesday
30th September

We are supposed to be mummers of the village and
Greg is anxious that I'm not recognised when I come
on later as Marcade, so a major make-up job is called
for. To hide my trademark baldy head, I wear a wig
as a disguise and have bright-green make-up applied
to my face. The green face recalls the pagan legend
of the green man of the forest, and although I worry
slightly that this verdant patina may actually draw more
attention to me, in combination with the hair it should
disguise me very effectively. Ahhh the wig ... hey-ho
it's been 20 years since such locks graced my bonce.
Onstage we work out how the dance will fit for there
are roots to be negotiated and also the step up to the
back of the stage where the paving has been lifted. Then
it's back to the dressing room for a read or some guitar
practice until I'm sent for.

In the afternoon my Marcade costume arrived having
been couriered over from Tiddington. It showed much
promise in the fitting and the final article certainly
didn't disappoint. Having been made for me it fitted
like a glove (if that's not mixing some kind of clothing

metaphor), the heavy layers of thick black fabric and the immaculate cut absolutely reflecting the gravitas and status of the character. As all good costumes do, it made me *feel* like a 16th-century French courtier. The role has its own pressure – it is a handful of lines but a massive moment in the play. I feel a little like the trumpet player in a symphony orchestra who has one vital fanfare to play right at the climax; if you muck it up there's no chance for recovery and an important moment in the story lost forever. In addition to the glorious cozzie I discussed some kind of make-up with the costume designer Katrina Lindsay. As well as some Walter Raleigh-esque facial hair I want to look pale, hollow-eyed, skull-like. Katrina gave the thumbs up to that idea although counselled caution; she didn't want me to look *too* skeletal … Fair enough … although not being the smallest of chaps I don't think there'd be much chance of that! Of course what she meant was that she didn't want my Marcadian pallor to look stylised as it would be out of kilter with the rest of the production. I've just realised I think that in this show I will actually spend more time in the wig and make-up room then I will on stage.

Back to the tech. I finally made my entrance for the final scene at about 5:00 and we were done by 6:00. Those of us involved in the interval show stayed on a little longer after a supper break to re-work the songs and dances in situ in the foyer, as it was closed to the public by this time, and we were finished by about 8:20.

W E'RE just about to open the 1st preview of Love's Labour's Lost and are in the middle of our final dress rehearsal. The tech was completed in record time and done and dusted by Tuesday evening. Whilst this is usual for a Swan show, it is unheard of for RST or Courtyard shows, which are usually technically much more complex. But Greg is very efficient at running techs plus this particular play has only nine scenes and no set changes, hence the world record.

We had our first dress run Wednesday afternoon, a careful canter through the play, typical of a first dress run in the theatre as we adjust to the space, lights music etc. Another first: after the dress we had yesterday evening off as well. Two evenings off in production week? It just doesn't happen.

Well rested with time on our side, today's final dress was in excellent shape – now we desperately need an audience. I have to say that there's a real sense of leaping into the unknown, as we aren't entirely sure how people will respond to this relatively unknown comedy. It is quite unlike *The Dream*, which is far more accessible as much of the humour springs directly from the action; it is also simpler linguistically and of course much more familiar, so in rehearsals we were able to enjoy the rough and tumble of the story. With *LLL* we've spent most of the rehearsal period trying to untangle the meaning and wit of the words so that the audience won't need to.

Tuesday 7th October

W E'RE in the middle of the preview period now and the audience response has been fantastic! The first preview was hysterical, though in notes the next day quite sensibly Greg warned us not expect the same reaction at the second preview as first-preview audiences in Stratford tend to be attended by RSC regulars who are keen to give their support to a new-born production. However, to our delight Greg was wrong and our second audience on the Friday was just as enthusiastic as the first! However he did warn us in notes on Saturday morning that Saturday audiences can be harder to please: they've paid a little more, will have tended to have booked further in advance and therefore have higher expectations. From experience I know that can be true, but happily he was wrong again and the response was as strong as ever. On Monday he didn't bother to warn us of the perils of a Monday night and it looks as though we've another hit on our hands.

Wednesday
8th October

T HE customary press-day ritual to take our mind off the critics, focus on the show and bond as a company. An afternoon vocal and physical warm-up then some text work with Cis and some final words from Greg. Then the distribution of good luck cards, flowers, wine and presents, and then ... the show itself.

The press performance got a great reception and I met my mum and dad (Pamela and Peter) who came up from Cheltenham for the occasion. They thought the production was delightful and joined us all for drinks and a buffet in the upper foyer afterwards and more drinks at The Duck after that. I resisted the temptation to quaff as much I did for the *Hamlet* press party and so was spared a cranium-busting hangover the next morning. Which was just as well because I had to get up early: a man was coming round with a big ladder to clear the gutters of our house before the winter ... oh the glamour of showbiz!

But never mind press nights and parties, what about rites of passage? The major event of the past few days was driving down to London to pick up my son Laurence and take him to Oxford University, where he is going to study music. His mum Shona and I are so very, very proud of him. Having helped set up his room in college it was very moving to leave him there, positively fizzing with excitement on the threshold of his adult life. It seems to be not so long ago that he was a tiny babe; now no longer a boy he's a bright, independent young man striking out on a fantastic voyage. I am reminded of a wonderful set of poems by Kahlil Gibran called *The Prophet*, one of which is about children; the first few lines seem particularly apt.

Your children are not your children.
They are the sons and daughters of Life's longing for itself.
They come through you but not from you,
And though they are with you, yet they belong not to you.
You may give them your love but not your thoughts.
For they have their own thoughts.

Autumn Anarchy and other stuff

Sunday 12th October

IT'S 25 years since the founding of the Friends of the RSC. As well as their undying loyalty as audience members this dedicated group support the RSC in many other ways, including helping to fund the supply of basic items that actors need in their digs to make their busy lives a little easier when they come to spend several months up here – e.g. kettles, duvets, furniture and the like. There was a bit of a celebratory do this evening. Greg gave a fine speech of appreciation, Tony (Sher) cut the cake and there was food, wine and fun. Quite a few of us actors mingled and the RSC choir sang some pieces, including my own four-part arrangement of Happy Birthday; well, I've got to do something during the first half of *Love's Labour's Lost* haven't I?

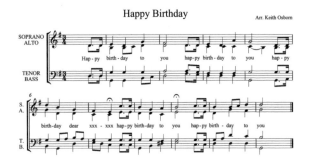

Happy Birthday

Arr. Keith Osborn

Saturday 18th October

A TRULY anarchic final scene in *Hamlet* tonight! After Osric's exit when all the Danish court enter for the final scene some furniture and props need to be brought on; I'm charged with bringing on the queen's

throne. I picked it up by the arms as usual and just
as I stepped out into the light onto the stage heard a
creak and a crunch and the right arm came away in my
hand. I managed to catch the main part of the throne
so that at least it didn't clatter to the floor drowning
out Claudius's first speech, but then it was one of those
split-second decisions: do I exit and dump the chair
offstage or go on with it as it is? I instantly decided not
to go off, as it'd look odd if only the king had a throne,
so on I went. That choice necessitated a further split-
second decision: what do I do with the broken arm? Do
I hang on to it, take it offstage or deposit it somewhere
at the back in the hope no one will see it? OR do I risk
trying to fix the chair in front of 1000 people without
any of them noticing? I glanced down at the severed
arm in my right hand and saw that the dowelling that
had joined the arm to the top of the chair leg hadn't
snapped. I might be able to bash it back in the hole IF
the same is true of the dowelling at the top end of the
leg itslef; if that dowelling has snapped there won't
be a hole to bash into and I'll have to think again...
The above thought process must've flashed through
my brain in the time it took me to take one step. I got
to the marks on the stage where the throne is to be
set and carefully put it down. Thankfully the entire
Danish court acted as a human shield and as discreetly
as I could I put the dowel rod-end onto the hole at the
top of the leg, took a deep breath and thumped it with
heel of my palm. Fortunately it snapped into place...
phew... crisis over. Then I started to cross to my
position on the other side of the stage upstage right. But
then it occurred to me that it may not be fully secure,
and I had visions of Gertrude, innocently leaning on the
arm only to be precipitated on to the stage as it came
loose. The nightmare vision of the queen of Denmark
rolling around on the floor, and the resulting loss of

dignity being entirely my fault, stopped me in my tracks and I returned to the courtiers upstage left. I whispered to Riann Steele who is a lady-in-waiting to warn the queen of the situation; she in turn whispered to Sam Dutton (gentleman-in-waiting) who was in a better position to inform Gertrude of the parlous condition of the throne. As I returned to my side of the stage I saw him deliver the message to the queen and the slight flicker in her eyes confirmed that she'd got it … mission accomplished!

Another mishap: in the middle of the big fight David's rapier blade snapped and the end flew off into space, creating mayhem. Peter De J valiantly came to the rescue and managed to get another one from the fallen sword rack upstage and hand it to him so that the fracas could continue safely, but where was the missing piece? It could be on stage and someone might slip on it and sustain an injury. As the fight continued and after it'd finished I scanned the floor but didn't spot the offending shard of metal anywhere. After the show it was never found so we assumed that it must've ended up in the audience. We were very lucky no one had been hurt, and I suspect that it ended up being taken home by someone as a souvenir.

Sunday 19th October I APPEARED at the Cheltenham Literary Festival today. Elizabeth Freestone, who I worked with when she was an assistant director on 'The Gunpowder' Swan season in 2005, is directing *The Tragedy of Thomas Hobbes* by Adriano Shaplin as part of the RSC London season. They were asked to talk about their collaborative process at the Cheltenham Literary

Festival, and as 'Green Company' were 300 miles away in Newcastle doing *The Taming of the Shrew* and *The Merchant of Venice* she asked me and Zoë Thorne to help present it. (By the by it should be noted by all theatrical trivia completists out there that Zoë T must be the first actress in theatrical history to play two Shakespearean Moths concurrently – the so-named fairy in *The Dream* and Don Armado's companion in *Love's Labour's*.)

To start it was the usual leisurely Sunday: coffee, papers, then a lunch of pot-roast guinea fowl with orange and white wine, a walk for Milly, followed by a cup of tea and cakey. Early evening Elizabeth picked me up from my front door, we quickly got to Cheltenham and huddled in the festival hospitality room to discuss what we're going to do. The only distraction was some delicious food and wine that'd been laid on (well it had been at least 3 hours since the guinea fowl). We were the last item in the entire festival, on at 8:30, and we had a respectable audience as Zoë and I read various drafts of scenes that Adriano had written. As a play it's fascinating and witty and I hope I can get to see the whole thing in London. My parents live in Cheltenham and came along to see what I was up to. We all shared a couple of glasses of wine after and then it was back to Alcester.

ALTHOUGH those moments of anarchy when props or furniture acquire lives of their own in order to try to bamboozle us actors can be quite scary, it has to be said that there is also a certain thrill of working together with one's colleagues to tame the unruly beasts when they run amok. There was another

Monday 20th October

occurrence, similar to Saturday's, in tonight's funeral scene at the point when Gertrude rushes to Hamlet to comfort him on his outpouring of grief and rage at Ophelia's death. She says:

> ... *This is mere madness;*
> *And thus a while the fit will work on him.*
> *Anon, as patient as the female dove*
> *When that her golden couplets are disclos'd,*
> *His silence will sit drooping ...*

As she started to move, Penny's brooch fell off her coat and skittered across the stage, coming to rest at my feet. This may sound trivial but anything left on stage unplanned is a potential hazard, even a small brooch, especially as there was about to be a fight close to a yawning grave into which ... it didn't bear thinking about. At first I thought that I'd simply bend down and pick it up, but quickly realised that as I was standing very close to the main action I was too exposed. It would've distracted from a very powerful and emotional part of the scene and invited the audience to think that Marcellus was a thief trying to steal the queen's jewels. So this time *I* became the human shield. I stepped over the offending item of jewellery as if reacting to the main action and stood as broad as I could in my bulky trench coat willing Sam Dutton, who I knew was behind me, to twig what I was doing and pick it up. The telepathy worked, Sam was once more the hero of the day, and the magic of ensemble demonstrated once again.

P OST-*LOVE'S Labour's* press night we're nearly
home and dry rehearsal-wise but for... yes you've
guessed it... UNDERSTUDY REHEASALS! These took
the usual pattern except that *LLL* is the production
in our season that has been picked for the *public*
understudy run, which we played today. These have
been a great success and have given audiences a sense
of the work that goes on behind the scenes to support
a show. Also most importantly they reveal the hidden
depths of the ensemble in that an actor who may only
have a dozen lines in the whole season may well be
playing a stonking great lead as an understudy. It is now
RSC policy that all company members must contribute
to the understudy process, thus in *Hamlet* we had
Patrick playing A Captain and Penny playing Cornelia
(the ambassador sent by Claudius to Norway). Penny
was so scrupulously thorough in her preparation for
this important role that she played her with a Swedish
accent to emphasise the character's international
credentials. In *Love's Labour's* we had David Tennant
giving his Forester and Nina Sosanya her Lady-in-
Waiting, but even with their assistance we still couldn't
avoid David Ajala playing Dumaine *and* Longaville and
Riann Steele playing Maria *and* Katherine meaning that
at points I'm afraid they did have to talk to themselves.
It is possible to make a virtue of this if it is done in such
a way as to include the audience in the game, which
was achieved on this occasion with the ubiquitous
change of hat and slight variation in the timbre of the
voice. It was also extra brownie points to David T who,
because Joe was ill, gamely volunteered at very short
notice to stand in as Marcade – now THAT's a trooper
for you!

We played to a good-sized house and the audience
were very appreciative. For the last time this season the
post-run tea and buns were taken in the green room.

Friday 24th October

SO now all official rehearsals are out of the way hip hip hooray! BUT, things are REALLY gearing up for the The Captain of Our Fairy Band gig. Over the last months we've developed some really very original interpretations of classic songs – modest, moi? – grabbing whatever rehearsal time we could, usually in our meal breaks in my dressing room, unless of course Sleepy Hollow was occupied. Our set of about 18 songs is more or less settled now, and we spent most of the day with amplifiers, microphones and a sound system set up in the RSC rehearsal rooms to practise with our various guest singers and instrumentalists from the company. We worked really hard all afternoon and by the end our brains completely scrambled. The gig's now set to go on the Tuesday 28th after *The Dream* after which we'll probably be international rock gods. We can't wait and I'm sure it'll be a storming night. Last night we had after-show drinks with the lovely people from Mace who are the contractors responsible for building the new theatre, and they're going to come along. They are great fun and absolutely passionate about the complex project they have undertaken. I've made some posters to advertise the gig and say what it's about (it's also a fund-raiser for Matt and Kev's New York Marathon run) so I went to Mace's site office to drop some off between band rehearsal and the show. What with the Mace contingent, undoubtedly quite a few RSC folk and anyone else who happens to be in the pub at that time there should be a good crowd.

If Music Be The Food ...

ZOË is stage-managing a concert of new music in The Courtyard, so I have most of the day to myself, excepting our faithful four-legged friend Milly. I take her for a long walk and already the winter crops are showing green through the brown-tilled fields. I go to the concert later, which is fantastic. The pieces are musical responses to Shakespeare – specifically *The Tempest* and Ophelia – by contemporary composers. They are interleaved with poems read by actors from our company (Penny, Minnie, Mark and Peter). The music is challenging and not what one would describe as easy listening but I love stuff like that.

TODAY is our final big rehearsal before the big gig tomorrow. Last Friday we went through the whole set calling each of our guest artistes in turn. It's a similar exercise today but we're paying especial attention to getting the core of the band really tight, so it's a long afternoon again for me, Rod, Sam and Mark, with our guests dropping in to do their numbers. It's *Hamlet* this evening so a long day too.

TODAY is THE day, we've practised for months for this and I'm very excited. We have one more rehearsal in the morning and then at teatime unplug the amps and mikes, load up the cars and set off for The Duck to set up and do a sound check. A space has been cleared for us in the restaurant at the back where we set up and try out a couple of song sections. Peter De J has come along and acts as an independent pair of ears to check the balance of the instruments out front. Then we push our equipment back into the corner to make way for the evening diners. I stick labels on collection buckets that we'll use to collect money for Kev and Matt's charity run and leave them at the pub for when people arrive.

That evening all through *The Dream* I'm thinking ahead, planning as hasty a departure as possible, going through my bass lines and the lyrics of the songs I'll sing. In one of my breaks I tune all the instruments so that we can make a quick get away as we need to start as near 11:00 as possible.

Curtain down and it's out of our Athenian weeds, into gig clothes and down to the pub with fiery quickness. There's already a great atmosphere and a good crowd; the building contractors from Mace have turned up and the place is buzzing. We hastily re-tune and re-check levels as best we can, pints of beer are brought to us and then it's time to go. We kick off with 'Where The Streets Have No Name' by U2, which I sing. I don't feel nervous but I'm a bit all over the shop, though I think I get away with it. It's a rabble-rouser that kicks things off to a lively start. Next up is Rod singing The Kinks classic 'Lola', and I'm able to relax a bit and just concentrate on the bass. Our first guest Ryan Gage sings Van Morrison's 'Brown Eyed Girl' – he's a very confident singer and struts his stuff magnificently. Next we slow down a bit with Sting's

'Fields of Gold' sung by Riann Steele and Peter De Jersey, followed by a couple of jazz standards, which is great for me as I get to wheel out a couple of walking bass lines I'm quite proud of. Cressida sings 'Cry Me a River' and Sam sings 'Nobody Knows' You by Jimmy Cox (our oldest song, written in 1923 and originally made famous by Bessie Smith). We start to crank things up again with 'Boogie Woogie Bugle' Boy, Riann Steele singing with Sam on harmonies and a scat-sung trumpet solo. Next up, 'Psycho Killer' by The Talking Heads performed with characteristic enthusiasm and charisma by Ricky Champ, who has specially written a rap that he performs in the middle eight. We finish off with an Eastern European take on 'Rapture' by Blondie – Zoë Thorne dead cool on vocals – and 'Play That Funky Music' sung by Andrea Harris who brings her New York sassiness to the end of the first half. We get a great reception and the buckets are passed round to collect the cash. It MUST be time for another beer!

The second set starts in a mellower mode. Rod sings 'Besame Mucho', a Latin-style song written by Consuelo Velázquez in 1940, featuring Sam Dutton on violin. Andrea returns to sing 'Little Wing' by Jimi Hendrix and Mark swaps his bongos for a guitar to sing a gorgeous version of James Taylor's 'Don't Let Me Be Lonely Tonight'. 'Dock Of The Bay' follows sung by Ryan, and then Peter sings a beautiful calypso version of 'Somewhere Over The Rainbow' by Israel Kamakawiwo Ole. We start to wind things up to the finale. I sing 'Every Little Thing She Does is Magic' and thankfully my bass-playing fingers and singing brain are now cooperating. Sam Dutton performs 'Jumping Jack Flash' with full Jagger swagger, then everyone is on their feet for our final number, 'Dance Tonight' by Paul McCartney. Naturally we are *compelled* to do an encore so it's volume up to 11 and we blast out Chuck Berry's

'Johnny B Goode'. Riann Steele, who is looking VERY merry, grabs the collection bucket and it goes round the dancing, singing crowd one more time; the evening ending with a classic rock 'n' roll flourish!

I'm very pleased with how the gig went. People have had a great time and are very complimentary, and even better it looks like there's quite a bit of dosh in the buckets. I carefully bag this up and tuck it deep down in the bottom of my bag. More drinks, we pack up the sound equipment and return it to the theatre having arranged with Barry at stage door to let us in. There's a post-gig party at Peter's place — more fun and errrm… more drinks, and I finally I crash at Sam Alexander's for the night.

Wednesday
29th October

I N the morning feeling somewhat weary I drive back to Alcester and count the money. We've raised £407.47, which is more than I thought, and I text the good news to Matt and Kev – by now en route to America for the event itself, if not already there. After the previous night's fun and frolics I feel pretty fatigued for the rest of the day. There's an Artists' Forum meeting at lunchtime, then I spend the afternoon checking and returning the sound equipment and the buckets lent by The Courtyard front of house.

It's *Hamlet* this evening, and in addition to the crowds of fans that festoon The Courtyard near showtime there's an entire TV outside broadcast unit. This is because tonight is the night of the National TV Awards and David is up for the gong for best drama performance. During Laertes farewell scene, just before Horatio and Marcellus take Hamlet to the battlements to see his father, the three of us usually have a little joke and a chat in the backstage area. This is one set of double doors away from the stage where the props tables and quick-change rooms are and where people working on the show quietly attend to their duties: moving costumes, preparing props etc. One wall is wallpapered with the pages and pages of documentation that comprise the Human Tissue Licence that's needed for André to make his appearance at Stratford; we'll need another one for London, a bargain at £250. Tonight, unable to ignore the satellite technology humming outside the theatre, Peter and I can't resist asking David if he's won. He smiles and quips 'If I were to tell you, I'm afraid I'd have to kill you'. But he *does* tell us that tonight's the night that he's going to announce his retirement as The Doctor ... WOW talk about hot off the press! We barely have time to digest this before we have to go through the pass door to the stage for our entrance.

The awards programme is timed so that David can make a live appearance in the interval and that's exactly what he does. Flanked on-screen by Ricky and Rob in their Switzer uniforms he accepts his award, and announces his departure from one of the most successful TV revivals ever. It's quite surreal to see what is happening outside only a few yards away indoors on the Green Room television!

After last night's triumph I'm completely knackered so go straight home after the show. My head hits the pillow, I close my eyes and the echoes of last night's music making quickly fade as I slip into a deep dreamless sleep...

The end is nigh...

1st November

NATALIE Walter threw a Halloween party after the show and transformed the front room of her cottage into a chamber of horrors! Fancy dress was of course essential.

5th November

IN 1613 Shakespeare's company, The King's Men, performed a play called *Cardenno* for King James I. We don't have this lost play in its original form but we do have what is claimed to be an adaptation of the original by Shakespeare and Fletcher, published by Lewis Theobald in 1728, called *Double Falsehood*; based on the *Cardenio* story in Cervantes *Don Quixote*. Way back in 2003 I took part in a rehearsed reading of this piece organised by Greg. He has quietly been developing the fragmented script and this afternoon, having worked on the play for a couple of days, we're reading another version edited by Greg. It's an absolutely fascinating project and I hope it comes to fruition in the future.

After the performance of *LLL* we had a bonfire party in the Ferry House garden.

6th November

*C*ARDENIO isn't the only script being developed. Over the last couple of months, often slaving over a hot laptop in the dressing room, Rod Smith has been writing a play of his own. It's called *Fourteen Mouthfuls of Air* and the idea came about from a discussion he had with Paul Englishby about modal jazz, which is where rather than improvise over a changing chord sequence, the soloist can choose any notes of the particular musical mode or scale that the piece is based on. The particular piece that inspired the play was 'So What' from Miles Davis' *Kinda Blue* album. For his play Rod has chosen 14 random words and written a dialogue of moods using only those 14 words with no regard to literal meaning, though he does indicate the emotions that the characters are feeling at various points. Slightly sadly, probably during the first half of *LLL* in between wig and makeup changes, I couldn't resist making a spreadsheet to analyse the relative frequency of these words. Fyi 'or' came first with 11.86% and 'collision' last with 4.31% and also ... no, that's probably enough of that. Rod has scheduled the performance for next Friday.

8th November

*A*ND tonight the star prize is... drum roll, drum roll, drum roll... ME! Well, Peter De Jersey and me to be precise. I've never been a prize before but it was a lot of fun. To explain, on the night of The Captain of Our Fairy Band gig in Stratford there was a huge gala fund-raising event for the RSC in London (stage managed by my very own Zoë ... which meant of course that she missed the greatest gig in the world ... doh!). By all accounts this gala involved fine foods and

wines, entertainment involving quite a few actors from
The Histories, and an auction hosted by David Tennant
(who would otherwise have been booked to sing '500
Miles' by The Proclaimers in aforesaid gig). Well, one
of the lots on offer at this auction was six tickets to
Hamlet, followed by dinner with two of the cast on
stage. As luck would have it the two ended up being
Peter and me. We were both a little nervous during
the show, it felt like we were going on a sort of weird
double blind date. Of course our slight anxiety was
unfounded and our guests were absolutely charming.
After the show we met for drinks and then took our
places on the stage, where a round table stood bathed
in a pool of light. We showed them round behind the
scenes and the conversation flowed, as did the wine.
They were passionate about the theatre, which was of
course reflected in the generosity of the donation they'd
made in order to secure their prize, and we had a very
jolly evening. I got a cab home; I sat back in my seat and
as it accelerated away from the glow of the town into
the darkness of the open road, it struck me that we had
but one week left in Stratford.

13th November IT'S the last *Dream* in Stratford tonight. Of course
it's part of our London season but we will miss
playing The Courtyard. Actually today is a double
Dream day, we have a matinee, and there is a camera
crew present making a documentary for Channel 4 who
want a flavour of what it's like just before curtain up.
We all try to be as normal as possible, ignore them and
act natural, but a degree of self-censorship is inevitable
and the jokes and banter are much cleaner than usual. I

must admit I could only stand the pressure for a couple of minutes and sought refuge in the wings, steadying my concentration for these final Stratford *Dreams*.

We got through the matinee fine, but last nights are funny things. While we all strive to make them as ordinary as possible as each scene passes it's hard to forget, given the transient phenomenon that theatre is, that that particular show will never be performed again: those words, moves, emotions gone forever. Of course they will live in people's memories but the visceral act of theatre will be no more, the last performance a metaphorical carpet to be rolled up and packed away in the mind. Having said that I consider myself to be a tough old stick and so determine to just get through it … which I did until the song at the end when Oberon and Titania bless the house of Theseus and Hippolyta:

> *Through the house give glimmering light*
> *By the dead and drowsy fire;*
> *Every elf and fairy sprite*
> *Hop as light as bird from briar;*
> *And this ditty after me*
> *Sing, and dance it trippingly.*

Peter sings this verse then Andrea as Titania summons up 'every elf and fairy sprite' to 'bless this place', at which point the rest of the cast appear amongst the audience with lanterns and reprise the song together as a round. It took us ages to get this right and it's a beautiful moment; Greg directed the song to be a kind of blessing of the theatre itself. As the words left my lips tough old stick turned into soppy old thing, my eyes smarted and a lump filled my throat as it hit me that our season here in this fantastic theatre was all but over. I recovered my composure and managed to finish the song... just. We got a standing ovation, flowers were thrown and *The Dream* was over.

Tonight was also the night of our end-of-season party in The Duck, but I just wasn't in the mood: it was too crowded and noisy, there were loads of people there that I didn't know who seemed to take over the place, and I'm afraid to say soppy old thing turned into grumpy old man and I went home.

14th November

THERE was a staff meeting with Michael Boyd and Vikki Heyward today to update everyone on next season and the building works, and to take any questions that people might have. It was very interesting. I must say next year's big ensemble project sounds brilliant – Shakespeare of course, but new writing as well and the opportunity for us actors to develop our own work: 'Actor's Anarchy' as Michael called it. I so want to be a part of it but we'll just have to wait and see. There are eight directors, all of whom will have their own people they will want to use, so it's going to be very difficult to get in. Ah well, one just has to remind oneself that there is a world elsewhere, other places to work and that one shouldn't expect to hang one's hat on one peg. Still...

Also today we performed Rod's masterpiece, *Fourteen Mouthfuls of Air*, in one of the large rehearsal rooms. We shared it with members of the company who loved its anarchic yet structured aesthetic. He filmed it and I can't wait to see it.

I T'S the very last day. The usual Saturday morning ritual – Zoë takes Milly to agility classes in Pershore very early, so I'm left with the paper, coffee and *Saturday Kitchen* on the telly. Zoë and Milly return, more coffee, a bit of a chat, I get ready and off I go for the last time this year trying to feel as normal as possible.

The matinee is *Love's Labour's Lost* and it really is the end for that show. At least *Hamlet* and *Dream* get a run in London, and I wonder whether *LLL* is a victim of there being no permanent RSC London base yet. Earlier in the year the producers tried to find a way for it to play in rep with *Hamlet* over Christmas at The Novello Theatre, but logistically it proved impossible, which means that Nina Sosanya leaves our happy band today. This is very sad: she's a lovely person and a fantastic Rosaline. Just as for *The Dream* on Thursday we try to make things as normal as possible – thankfully I don't have another wobbly moment. The response is fabulous and now it's two down, one to go.

Hamlet is our final Courtyard performance. Before and during the show people start to clear their desks. First-night cards that've had their places all season blue-tacked around mirrors are taken down, the paraphernalia of dressing room life dismantled and packed away. We of the Senior Common Room have had a great few months together and will inevitably be split up amongst the smaller dressing rooms at The Novello. Over a long season relationships develop and the company bonds over time, even more so when you share a dressing room as you spend a lot more time together. We've had some great laughs.

The response to the final *Hamlet* is STUPENDOUS – we ARE rock stars; screams, cheers, flowers, the lot and then the season is over. Off we go backstage where we say goodbye to Suzi, who is leaving the show tonight.

Michael Boyd was in with his daughter and has asked us to gather so that he can thank us all for our hard work – not just the actors but the whole team, including crew, stage management, company manager and a particular thank you to Greg. It is a very moving tribute after which we disperse to get back into our civvies for the last time. We of the Senior Common Room thank our dresser, Michelle, give her a present for all her hard work, and crack open some champagne as we do the final tidy up. Make-up into boxes, rails of costumes and wigs all packed up to be taken away in preparation for transport to London. Au revoirs are said to those heading off home into the night tonight, and the rest of us go to the pub for a final drink. But before leaving I can't resist going back on to The Courtyard stage once more. It's still set for *Hamlet*'s final scene, thrones and sword racks strewn and flowers, tributes thrown onto the stage by the audience, still had lying where they landed. The auditorium is empty and silent but for the echoes of the season's memories that reverberate in my mind, alongside the inevitable questions. Will I ever be here again? Is this the last time? Who knows? Uncertainty, famously, is the actor's lot and we just have to accept it. With that thought I turn on my heel, back through the backstage area, pick my bags up from the dressing room and head off for a beer. I bump into Greg on the way to the pub, which he has just left. 'Just said a final farewell to the theatre' I say. He smiles and replies 'Oh I don't think that's a final farewell for you is it?' I laugh and resist the temptation to read anything into his cryptic response; we have a quick hug and say goodbye. One beer in The Duck, more goodbyes, then into the car and my own short journey home to Alcester.

NOW IS THE WINTER ...

Capital investments ...

WE start our season at The Novello tomorrow morning so I have to leave home and go to London tonight. This is in contrast to most of my fellow actors who have returned home having spent half the year in Stratford. Post-Courtyard we've had a whole fortnight off, which I've spent relaxing at home walking the dog, practising my guitar, cooking … bliss! I visited my parents in Cheltenham for one night, which was very nice; I came back with a load of windfall Bramleys and made a batch of chutney, which should be ready for consumption in the New Year. I also had two guitar lessons with my teacher Chris Hadley in King's Norton. He gave me quite a bit to practise, some classical stuff and some flamenco, which is great for variety is the spice of life and realistically I probably won't see him again until I'm back after Christmas. Having procrastinated as far as I possibly could I also did my tax. Not much fun you might think – scrabbling through a shoebox full of receipts, putting them in order to send to my accountant and entering them into a spreadsheet on my computer. Sad as it may sound though, I must confess that I quite enjoy it; I think its something to do with making order out of chaos, and not forgetting the geek factor of course. You see, I've done this brilliant spreadsheet with formulae and everything and … perhaps I should get out more.

For today, we have a fairly low-key Sunday in an attempt to normalise my imminent departure: the customary morning coffee and papers, a long walk, and a lovely roast lamb from Reg Phillips our local butcher. Around teatime I pack a rucksack with a week's worth of clothes, my computer, guitar and bike and load up the car. Whilst I'm very excited about our London

season it is with a heavy heart I say goodbye to my
beloved, but we stoically remind each other of the fact
that I'll be back Saturday night, and that being apart is
an inevitable consequence of our shared life in showbiz.

I leave early evening so as not to get to my
destination too late. It's dark and the drive down is
pretty grim on account of a surprising amount of traffic
and rain. I am returning to stay with Philip, so at least
it's home from home from the start and not some
anonymous digs. I know that he's away for the week
working in Chichester so I probably won't see him until
next week. When *finally* I arrive I unpack the car and
text Zoë to let her know I'm back safe. The familiar
night arrival ritual of food, red wine, crap television
and bed, in readiness for the relatively early start next
morning.

I WAKE up early... too too early, you know one of
those wake-up-at-five-and-unable-to-go-back-to-
sleep situations the only possible conclusion to which
is finally getting to sleep at seven o'clock just in time
for the alarm to go off at seven-thirty. Drowsily I drag
myself out of bed and have a quick cup of tea, which I
sup while listening to *The Today Programme* on Radio
4, my preferred way of easing my way into the waking
hours of the morn. Now only half asleep, I bathe, don
my bike gear and set off to brave the rush hour traffic.

The crisp morning air, noise and general chaos of
London soon blow the cobwebs away as I hurtle down
the Camden Road into the city centre. I played The
Novello a couple of years ago when we took *Antony and
Cleopatra* to London, so it is with a sense of déjà vu that

Monday 1st December

185

I weave my way through the traffic, dodging taxis, buses and pedestrians; how different to the Warwickshire country lanes I've become so accustomed to. I arrive in good time and go to my dressing room, which I will share with Ewen. It's small but cosy and we have the added bonus of having our own shower, which we somewhat cruelly point out to whoever comes in, eliciting the standard response: 'You bastards, how did you manage that?' The company are called to the stage and everyone picks up where they left off with smiles and laughter and stories of whatever adventures were had in the holiday – it's almost like starting a new school term. Introductions to the Novello staff and crew are made next, and then we kick off yet another technical rehearsal. The transition from a thrust stage to a proscenium arch will require some adjustments, plus a couple of new design elements have been added and the way the set works is different. For example, rather than being wheeled on from the back, the entire assemblage of thrones, steps, Corinthian columns etc that is the set for the throne room for the play-within-the-play scene is flown in from the flys like a gigantic spaceship. This is an impressive sight, and some of us think that Patrick and Penny should be flown down on it for their entrance, but it's probably not in keeping with the rest of the production. As well as adjustments to what goes on onstage the backstage area is much smaller too, so we need to sort out where quick changes are done, how furniture is moved on and off, how we get from one side of the stage to the other and so on. In fact the stage-left wing at The Novello is practically non-existent, only about a metre deep, meaning that great care is required when exiting in that direction to avoid smashing into a brick wall.

It's interesting going from a thrust stage to a proscenium arch. Exciting and dynamic as The

Courtyard stage is, it is very challenging to play. The
audience aren't all viewing a picture in a frame – I
suppose its like a kinetic sculpture park – and in staging
or 'blocking' a scene some actors are inevitably going
to have their backs to some sections of the audience
and obstruct the view of others. No such problems
arise in a proscenium: the audience are all looking
in the same direction; therefore the performers only
have one direction to worry about being seen from.
In that respect it is simpler to play. I'd be interested
to know how the *Romeo and Juliet* company who have
been on tour, now in Stratford, have found the opposite
adjustment – proscenium to thrust.

We begin at the end of the play as Terry rejigs the
fight. This'll save time later when we get to the scene
proper, and also means that if there's some hitch that
prevents us from finishing the tech, he's gone through
it with David, Ed and the rest of us at least once in the
new venue.

Luckily no such hitch occurs today, we all know
the production and each other so well now, plus the
London crew and stage management – including our
new Stage Manager Amelia Ferrand-Rook – are so
incredibly efficient that we whip through pretty quickly
without any major problems and get within a whisker of
the interval, well over half the total playing time, by the
end of the day.

Tuesday
2nd December

WE pick up where we left off – Patrick's speech in the chapel 'O my offence is rank…' and David's 'Now might I do it pat… and now I'll do it', then blackout, interval and the longest caesura in theatrical history!

We gallop our way through the rest of the play and, true to Greg's legendary deftness at technical rehearsals, we manage a dress rehearsal starting at 5:30. Having spent a lot of the tech watching Patrick for any changes, I watch as much of the dress as I can; the show sits very comfortably in the Novello and it looks wonderful. Hurrah, we're finished by 9:30 and it's off to the pub for a swift couple of pints, on my bike and up the hill to Islington for an earlyish night in anticipation of our first preview tomorrow. A slight worry, David has had a little twinge in his back, but he's a trooper and soldiers on as it's probably nothing serious.

London previews…

Wednesday
3rd December

THE day of our first preview. We aren't called until the afternoon so have the bonus of a lie-in. We start the afternoon's work by practising all the scene changes, giving the new London crew another crack at them, and the new band get the chance to practise some of the music cues. A cup of tea and then Greg gives some notes and rallies the troops for our first London performance. London audiences are subtly different to Stratford audiences and can seem harder to

please, so it'll be interesting to see how the response to
the play varies.

As with Stratford there are the same pre-show calls.
For my song call I have to descend into the very bowels
of the building as the band rooms are under the stage.
They're tiny and I have to crick my neck when standing,
which makes warming up a sitting-down operation as I
can't sing the Miserere with a crooked neck as it tenses
the muscles and doesn't permit a clear passage of air.

Our first Novello preview goes very well and in the
event the response didn't seem that different, but most
importantly all the changes we've made so far work.
Greg is clearly moved as he says how proud he is of the
cast, the crew and the whole team over the tannoy at
the end of the show for the seamless transition to the
new space. The Novello throws a drinks party in one of
the bars to welcome us and christen the start of our run
here.

ANOTHER morning off and we're called to fine-
tune the show based on what we learnt from last
night. Tim Mitchell has tweaked some of the lighting
in the morning and we do a little more re-blocking to
mould the physical life of the show to suit The Novello.
Amelia gives tomorrow's call, which is not until mid-
afternoon; bang on course when mounting a new show
in that if all is well the calls tend to get later and later
through the preview period.

The second preview is another step forward in the
recalibration of the show.

Friday 5th December

DESPITE having the morning off I have a busy day ahead of me. It's the last day of Laurence's first term at Oxford and I have to drive up to collect most of his stuff as there's too much for him to carry. I've warned stage management I'm heading out of town but I should be back in time for notes at 3:30 barring major traffic or break down. It's a beautiful bright morning: the low winter sun illuminates the all-too-familiar M40 as it snakes through the landscape, over and down through the Stokenchurch cutting and a wonderful view of the county of Oxfordshire stretches before me as I speed down the hill.

I get to Laurence's college just after midday. He seems very happy and things seem to've gone well for him. He's travelling back by train later in the day but I'm on a tight schedule so we load his trunk and instruments into the car, have the briefest of chats and I have to turn around and go straight back to London. He's very sweetly bought me a sandwich for my lunch, which I eat en route.

When I get back to London I unload his things at his flat, swap my car for my bike and set off for the Novello. I get there in good time and notice that as we all meet for notes in the auditorium there are some missing faces. I sit next to Andrea in the theatre stalls and she tells me she's on standby to go on for Penny, as Penny is unwell and might not make the performance. And someone else is missing… before Greg starts to share his thoughts on last night's show he informs us that David's back is very painful and he is resting in his dressing room. Furthermore, whilst intending to start the show he may not be able to complete it – cue collective intake of breath – so Ed is on standby too;

talk about sorrows not coming single spies. Notes continue as normally as possible and some even finer tuning is tuned.

We have a fight call before every show at 6:15. David has emerged from his room and has taken some powerful painkillers, which he confesses have made him feel 'a bit pissed'. His movement seems a little restricted but not too bad as we go through the fight, although I worry that the painkillers might mask further damage. Penny has recovered sufficiently well that she can go on too, armed with cold remedy and a mountain of tissues.

The strangeness of the situation hits me as I head down from my dressing room after beginners is called; the evening is balanced on a knife-edge. David's wonderful wit and quickness of thought is manifest in the sharpness and dexterity of the physical life he brings to Hamlet, which he sustains throughout the play. It's stating the bleedin' obvious but Hamlet is a very demanding part indeed, mentally and physically. Also never mind the show, he must be in a lot of pain for there to be any doubt about him performing. That said, Ed is very well prepared and if we have to stop then so be it – it's only a play and David's health is far more important. In the wings, waiting to go on for the first scene, I try to forget the situation and concentrate on the job in hand. All goes well and he turns in a great performance as ever, sitting down or moving around whenever he needs to ease his back, but nothing the audience would've noticed. After the show we're told that there'll be no Saturday call apart from for the performance. Hopefully this'll mean that David can rest up all day and be on the mend for the evening.

**Saturday
6th December**

LAURENCE cooks me lunch, there's a first! I was going to take him out but he insisted. He makes an excellent tuna pasta and we have a proper natter this time before he goes off to catch up with his London mates.

I go into town early for some retail therapy – which usually involves CDs – then get to The Novello in time for some nosh and the fight call. David is sitting on the stage. 'How's the back?' He shakes his head 'Not great.' It hasn't changed since yesterday.

Again we get through the play, in the last scene I can see that he is in quite some discomfort. Well it's the end of the week – surely a day off and rest will have him bouncing back right as rain on Monday.

After the performance I set off home to Alcester, on my bike I get and off I go. No, I'm not riding all 100+ or so miles to Alcester, but in order to get back as soon as possible after the Saturday performance I've worked out a sort of relay event. I cycle to my car parked just north of the centre of town where parking rates are cheaper (the end of the job is getting nearer and nearer so I'm getting increasingly skinflint financially), then off with the front wheel, bike in the back, fire up the engine and I'm on my way home. There's some quite boring traffic for some bridgeworks near Acton but after that its plain sailing and I'm back by 1:15 in the morning ... red wine, munchy food, crap telly ...

Sunday 7th December

A WHOLE day at home… hurrah! And I'm not called until Monday afternoon so I don't need to head off into the night this week, but will leave after lunch tomorrow. There is a small voice at the back of my head reminding me that we still don't know what's wrong with David's back. He's going for some tests but he's a fit bloke and basically I'm an optimist, so I'm sure all will be well.

When sorrows come ...

A FTER recharging the batteries and a day at home it's back to London today. I say goodbye to Zoë as she leaves for work (until her next stage management assignment she's got some temp work in the RSC producers' office). I have a couple of household things to attend to, after which I'll have a bite to eat, walk the dog and drive off. But then the phone rings – its Zoë: 'You're going to have a very interesting show tonight... David is off. His back is still very bad and so Ed will be on tonight.' Wow! Katie Vine our new Company Manager for London rings around midday to confirm the situation. This means that I may need to return early, so I walk Milly immediately just in case. I take the route round the back of Oversley Woods. Yesterday there was quite a frost and Milly got terribly confused when she tried to drink from an iced-over puddle. In fact it quite freaked her out and she did some mad running round in circles typical of the slightly crazily playful temperament of the boxer breed. Today though the ground is sodden, the sky a luminous grey. It's our London press night tomorrow; I guess that they're sending Ed on today so that David will be fighting fit for that.

Monday
8th December

It transpires that I won't be needed in the afternoon, just for the usual show call. So after the walk I pack a couple of things and prepare to leave. I've managed to exhaust Milly so she barely raises an eye from her slumber as I pat her on the head and head off.

I have a pretty horrendous journey back. I decide to go the pretty way via Banbury; big mistake, as there's an accident and I get held up for quite a few minutes. Then when hit to London it's very slow going. Eventually I get to my parking spot, park the car, get on my bike and pedal like mad to get to the theatre in time. To my annoyance – today of all days – I'm five minutes late. The company are called for the fight sequence at the end of the play.

The atmosphere at the Novello is electric. Terry King is taking Tom Davey – normally Guildenstern, but tonight Laertes – and Ed through the fight simplifying it where necessary, safety as ever being the priority in what is bound to be a very strange evening, at the climax of which Ed will be fighting himself. Ed is looking good but confesses that he is a little nervous. It'd be quite nerve-wracking enough to go on for the biggest Shakespeare role in the canon in an RSC production in the West End, but there's extra pressure in that this particular production of *Hamlet* has attracted an awful lot of attention. A fair portion of the audience will have come especially to see David; how will they react when they realise that he's not performing? Notices have been put out in the foyer and Greg is going to make a speech just before the start, so at least they will be primed.

Leading up to the half everyone rallies around Ed in particular, but also the knock-on understudies: Tom of course, Ricky Champ – Lucianus (the villain in *The Murder of Gonzago*) now Guildenstern, and Rob Curtis – Fortinbras which he will retain with extra added

Lucianus. The other company member who won't be appearing tonight is André, as Ed hasn't had a chance to rehearse with him.

It's beginners and it's buzzing backstage. Greg prepares to go out and speak to the audience. Front-of-house clearance is given which means that Amelia can start the ball rolling. Greg takes a deep breath and steps out into the light; we listen in the dark wings to what unfolds. He introduces himself and explains, insofar as he can, David's situation, continuing: '…but we are very lucky to have Edward Bennett who will be giving his debut as Hamlet tonight.' At this point a huge cheer erupts from the audience followed by applause; we all cheer and indeed are cheered backstage as quite clearly the audience are on our side. Greatly relieved, Greg comes back through the wings. There are smiles and pats on the back as the usual mobile phone announcement is made, the lights go into performance mode and it's curtain up.

Ed is brilliant – he grabs hold of Hamlet, makes it his own and plays a blinder, getting a well-deserved standing ovation at the end and applause from us too. Astonishingly, presumably on account of that rocket fuel commonly known as adrenalin, he has also taken nearly 15 minutes off the playing time! Greg is on the tannoy as we get changed and is fulsome in his praise of Ed in particular, the other understudies and our teamwork. He also tells us that the position on David is unclear and we'll have to wait for tomorrow to find out whether he'll be on for press night; I find it hard to believe he won't.

PRESS night and it is confirmed that David is off. Poor guy, he must be devastated, as must Greg. However well we're all doing to steady the ship, especially Ed, the production's evolution over the months in Stratford – let alone the many more months of planning pre-rehearsal – now gives way to unavoidable emergency measures. Ed has an hour's rehearsal solus with Cressida then the difficult closet and nunnery scenes in the afternoon with Penny and Minnie, and finally we consolidate the play scene and final scene. Just before the pre-show run of the fight, Greg gathers the whole company to the stage for a final rallying call. At beginners he goes on and speaks to the press audience before curtain up as he did last night, and again we're relieved to hear resounding cheers out front. Then it's all systems go and we cry god for *Hamlet*, Edward and us all!

Press night couldn't have gone better in the circumstances. Ed is brilliant again, we all sing from the same hymn sheet, there's another standing ovation and as we make our way to the after-show party we're all delighted and relieved that it went so well.

The party is in the magnificent foyer and bar of Drury Lane theatre just over the way, where I meet my agent Sarah Barnfield who has brought Toby Whale, a casting director. I know Toby from some years back and it's great to see him again. He says he'll be in touch in the New Year, hopefully with some film or television work. Yes, at this stage of the season with just a few weeks to go thoughts turn to what happens next, and whilst I'd love to come back for the ensemble season next year I've a sinking feeling that it's not going to happen. I must remind myself that, despite the disappointment, there really *is* a world elsewhere...

Anyway back to the party. The wine flows freely and there's 'bowl food', which are Lilliputian helpings of main meals served in a small bowl (e.g. fish and chips, thai green curry, beef stroganoff to name but a few). They were a huge hit at the post-show parties in Stratford and are again tonight. I bump into quite a few friends who I haven't seen for yonks and have a jolly good time. The party ends about 1:00am and as is compulsory for London first nights, some of us go in search of one final nightcap. Unfortunately we can't find anywhere open so, having been here many times before in London, I treat myself to a taxi home at the end of a long and extraordinary day, fall into bed and sleep like a baby.

Post dramatic press reorder...

FOLLOWING the relief of getting through press night (the reviews were mostly excellent) we learned that David's back was worse than hitherto realised. Following tests it transpired that he needed to have an operation and wouldn't return before Christmas. This was a real blow as we'd all hoped that although he'd missed his own press night that he'd be off for a few days and come back in a blaze of glory. How disappointing for us not to get our friend back, and for him to be unable to return. All we could do was deal with the situation and our own feelings and get on with the job, reminding ourselves that it's still a fantastic show. Ed is wonderful and has gained more confidence with each performance.

After press night we had a couple of days of understudy rehearsal in preparation for a full understudy run on the Tuesday 16th December. These were slightly stranger than usual in that the excitement and trauma of the week had left Ed so exhausted that we had to rehearse quite a bit without him; clearly his well-being had to be protected, because if *he* was off we'd have to cancel.

Saturday
13th December

AN extraordinary moment tonight when Laertes returns to confront Claudius about Polonius' death. Tom stormed on supported by our offstage vocals as his rebellious hordes and threatened Patrick with the revolver as usual, then as he threw off Penny as Gertrude who tries to calm him down, somehow he lost his grip and dropped the gun which slid across stage coming to rest at Patrick's feet. There was a slight pause … then the scene continued. It was electric – neither Patrick nor Tom tried to retrieve the gun, which stayed where it was until the very end. When it's clear that Laertes' emotional devastation at seeing Ophelia's madness has incapacitated him, Claudius knows that he has him in his power. At this point Patrick slowly picked the pistol up, walked over to Tom and with 'And where the offence is, let the great axe fall' calmly handed it back to him. It was brilliant, victory snatched from the jaws of poltergeist props, absolutely telling the story of Claudius' confidence that Laertes is broken, and a bit of stage business it must be tempting to keep.

MONDAY morning and we started the understudy tech without Ed, with Cressida standing in. The hope was for Ed to be fit for the actual run on Tuesday, and in the event, at the end of the afternoon, we were told that he although *he* was happy to do the run even if he had to do it half-throttle, the RSC had decided that the risk was unacceptable. We were asked whether we wanted to do the run the next day with Cressida or at a later date. I very quickly expressed my desire to do it asap in case I had to go on for Patrick. Some people didn't want to, but the consensus was that it would be a good idea to do it; I sensed that for the first time in the entire job that company morale was at very low ebb. To my great irritation it was further decided that no one in the business would be allowed in to see it. After the Stratford understudy run a lot of us had been looking forward to doing it in London, and my agent had worked hard over the weeks to get some casting directors to see me as the king and Rod as Polonius; clearly as the end of the job was creeping ever closer this was an opportunity that might've opened some doors. Clearly this was not now going to happen; what was going to be a bit of an event was now quickly turning into a damp squib. Also my parents were very sweetly coming all the way from Cheltenham to see me. I tried to contact them to put them off but they were already on their way.

Tuesday
16th December

THE day of the understudy run and what a strange beast it was. I hadn't been able to contact my parents and when they arrived at the stage door they were nearly turned away having been told that they wouldn't be allowed to see it. They'd come a long way and this burst the bubble of the anger and frustration I'd felt for the last couple of days. I insisted that they be allowed in as I really couldn't see what harm professionally or otherwise would come of it for anyone. The situation was resolved with five minutes to go – not exactly textbook preparation for a run – and they were shown to the auditorium. Cressida read in as Hamlet and went through the motions movewise. She did brilliantly, the run went as well as it could under the circumstances, and I was quite relieved to've played Claudius in this new environment. More importantly I sensed that it had helped us recover our morale and me my own disappointment. Michael Boyd saw it and thought it was extraordinary; he wondered whether this was the beginning of a whole new theatrical form – voice-over theatre where you just had the set and actors voices… I *think* he was joking…

Christmas 2008

ALL rehearsals, runs etc done for *Hamlet*, we just had the show to do in the lead up to Christmas, which was just as well as there was thus time for the dreaded Christmas shopping. I'm HOPELESS at it. Christmas shopping for me is wandering around crowded shops desperately hoping that the ideal presents for friends and family will leap out and declare themselves as perfect solutions to my yuletide retail confusion. What usually happens is that I find myself getting more and more annoyed and frustrated as I develop a sort of blindness where nothing seems to be remotely right. 'Make a list' advises Zoë. Well, that did help a little, and I managed to get it all done in time for posting. We only had Christmas Eve and Christmas Day off and a show on Boxing Day. After the show on the 23rd I drove back to Alcester for our short, sweet Christmas break. Zoë had organised everything brilliantly – food, tree, decorations – it's great being married to a stage manager. Christmas Eve was spent in final preparations for the day itself. In the evening we went to the early evening 'Children's Service' in St Nicholas church and sang some carols, then went to the pub with our next door neighbours and a couple of their friends for beers. Post-pub it was home for steak sandwiches – quick and simple in anticipation of the major cooking operation that defines Christmas Day in this country.

Having been flooded out last year we woke on our first Christmas morning in our house lit low by a bright, sharp winter sun. I ventured out with Milly whilst Zoë prepped the lunch. We'd invited my parents over to stay and our friend Gabs Sanders, an RSC stage manager, one of Zoë's best friends who lives nearby. Christmas day was tremendous fun and over all too quickly. Before I knew it I was back in the car and heading to London. I gave Ed a lift back as he'd been visiting his father who lives in Broadway fairly nearby.

We got back to London in plenty of time for the show, after which Sam Dutton had organised a 'Secret Santa' and a Christmas tree. We all opened our presents and drank some Boxing Day bubbly – I got a bottle of red wine… hic hic hurrah!

Leading up to New Year we were in show mode only – no more rehearsals and the day free, which after all the drama of the last few weeks was very welcome. On

New Year's Eve we had a matinee and as we had a show New Year's Day it wasn't worth driving home. After the show some of us went for a couple of beers, but I was a feeling very under the weather with man-flu so was compelled to have an early night. After a bite to eat with some of the company near the theatre, I cycled up to Islington and was asleep by 10:30, seeing out 2008 in slumberland.

■

Happy New Year!

HAVING had a cold-enforced too, too virtuous New Year's Eve I woke up in 2009 hangoverless and feeling much better if a little low. I'd been brooding on the fact that I still hadn't been approached about next year's Stratford season, and my tenuous hopes had by now become so threadbare that they'd finally snapped. I was certain as can be that I was not going to be asked to the party.

To make sure I'd conquered my cold I spent most of the day in a state of inertia, made phone calls to family and friends to wish them the salient greeting universally exchanged on 1st January and generally loafed about to save my energy for the evening's trip to Elsinore. The show was good, although the prop newspaper (used in the closet scene by Hamlet to chide his mother, comparing the picture on the cover of Patrick as Old Hamlet with his 'eye like Mars to threaten and command' to that of a bedside photo of Patrick as Claudius 'like a mildewed ear') flapped open at one point to reveal a large headline about Manchester United football team in the middle, the audience can't have seen but no doubt more anonymous insides will be chosen before tomorrow.

There had been a rumour that David may be back for the last week of the run, and at the end of this evening it was confirmed and we would indeed be rehearsing with him the next day with a view to him *possibly* doing the show on Saturday.

THE plan for the day was to go through all David's scenes to ascertain where we might have to adjust stuff physically – to take account of his back, which was still healing after the operation, and also simply to give him a chance to go through the lines again with us after three and a half weeks out. There were obvious places that needed rethinking, like the fencing at the end and the graveyard tussle, but there are always things one forgets so its best to go through the lot.

Peter and I were called first to re-rehearse the battlement scenes with him at 2:00. It was great to see him again, he seemed quite cheery and on good form, all things considered, having had a weird old Christmas and was clearly looking forward to getting back in the saddle. I asked him if he might be on tomorrow and he laughed, 'I don't know if I'm going to get through the afternoon yet.' Basically the brief was that he had to move slower, couldn't bear any loads and violent physical contact should be avoided. To that end we concentrated on the bit when Hamlet struggles with Horatio and Marcellus as they try to stop him following the ghost. Hitherto we physically pulled and

Friday 2nd January

pushed David away to protect him from the spectral
presence of Old Hamlet, but now we were required
to bring all our mime skills to bear, barely touching
him and letting him react as if we were pulling him
about; an interesting exercise and I think it was just as
convincing as actually man-handling him. After Peter
and I had done our scenes with him, he rehearsed,
amongst others, the nunnery, players' and closet
scenes, and at the end of the day we did the big fight
scenes mentioned above. Well he DID get through the
afternoon and a rehearsal was called for the next day ...
so far so good.

On the face of it, it looked like tonight might be Ed's
last performance as Hamlet. He'd grown and grown
over the three and a half weeks he'd been playing the
role and had done a fantastic job; we all joined in with
the audience and applauded him at the curtain call. At
the end of the show Amelia announced that there was
a call Saturday afternoon to work with David again but
that we weren't to tell anyone in case the press got hold
of it, and as yet we were still not 100% certain of his
return.

Saturday 3rd January

WE weren't called until late afternoon when
we had another look at the graveyard and
final scenes, David had suffered no ill effects from the
exertions of the day before and so he was definitely
back, at this stage strictly on a show-by-show basis but
hopefully for the final week.

At beginners we all gathered in the wings as Denise
Wood our producer went on stage to deliver the
good news. She introduced herself and then coolly

announced with great aplomb: 'Tonight, the role of
Hamlet will be played by... David Tennant,' at which
point an unbelievable cacophony of wild cheers and
screams worthy of any set of fans at a rock concert
erupted in the auditorium. This subsided into a loud
chatter drowning out the mobile phone announcement.
We who were about to go onto the battlements prayed
that they would settle or our job would become very
difficult. Fortunately things calmed down and away
we went. It was quite a strange show I couldn't but
help checking that David was ok in our scenes, but the
evening was a triumph and David was brilliant and
as fresh as a daisy. True, he was a little slower moving
about the stage, but seeing as he's such a naturally
speedy guy anyway I dare say no one would've noticed.
There were cheers at the end and as I went to leave the
theatre I popped my head round his dressing room door
to say well done and check how he was. He smiled and
said that he was fine though might ache a bit tomorrow.

A S Zoë had come up to London last Sunday to start
rehearsals for the new season on Monday, I hadn't
done the helter-skelter bike/car relay back to Alcester
but had met her from the station on Sunday evening.
Off she went bright and early Monday morning to
set things up for the new company (bah! They'll
never manage without me!). There were no adverse
consequences backwise arising from David's return on
Saturday, so I had a lazy day and went in for the first
show of our last week of *Hamlet*.

It was a great week and David was extraordinary.
Despite his enforced absence his performance had got

Late Saturday
10th January

even better, almost as if making up for lost time. It was wonderful to finish with the company complete. We counted down the last few performances and on Saturday night over a post-show glass of wine said goodbye to more of our merry band. Greg gave a speech reminding us as to what an extraordinary journey *Hamlet* had been: from the first day of rehearsal when we were agog as we set eyes on the skull of André Tchaikowsky, the talented pianist who had bequeathed his cranium to the RSC to appear as Yorick; to the hoards of Trekkies and Dr Who fans who thronged around the theatre in Stratford and London; to the trauma of David's back, his recovery and return. Having had one small beer I said my own goodbyes to Patrick, John, Oliver, Penny and David and set off for the journey home. Now, thundering back through the darkness of the motorway, I feel a wave of melancholy at the fact that our *Hamlet* has ended, to sleep no more and but for the clamour of many happy memories the rest but silence.

■

The true beginning of our end ...

Monday 12th January

WE of the Blue Company gather to commence the final leg of our journey together. Those who weren't in *Hamlet* return – Joe, Kathryn and Natalie – and the group is now the original one that first met nearly a year ago in a chilly rehearsal room in Islington. As it's been six weeks since we last did *The Dream* we're called for a line run in the afternoon. There's tea and

biccies in the Warldorf Bar at The Novello as we sit
in a circle in a niche that looks out high over London
and recite the play through without any major glitches,
although there's the odd dry that invites some good-
humoured ribbing from the rest of the cast. Having
gone through the play, we revisit the 'Philomel' with
Julian our Musical Director, and our day's work is
done, for tomorrow 'tis the tech. With the luxury of an
evening off I have a pint in the pub then meet Zoë in
Highgate to go for some scran. We're grateful for this
night off as although we work for the same company
and live in the same house in London, we hardly
ever see each other. She gets up early to rehearse in
Clapham and leaves me completely comatose. I go to
work in the evening before she gets home and return
after midnight when *she* is completely comatose.

O UR final tech and the routine is as for *Hamlet*, Tuesday 13th January
adapting the Courtyard staging for the
proscenium arch of The Novello. Little is different for
me except that, as the distance from dressing room to
stage is much further, I need to change to and from
Egeus and Fairy in the quick-change area backstage,
which for us chaps is a line of chairs stage right. At
The Courtyard, I merely tripped along the backstage
corridor to my dressing room, changed and returned
to the stage in good time. Here at The Novello the
distance is probably about the same but mostly vertical
in that there are about a million, well 64 steps to climb,
which is a right pain at the best of times and worse if
you get to the stage and realise that you've forgotten
something. It's a long climb back up again.

Friday 16th January

A S we might've expected we got through the technical in good time and had a dress rehearsal Wednesday night. Last night was our first preview, which we thoroughly enjoyed, as the audience seemed to too, we met the following afternoon for notes with Greg. It was all very buzzy as we gathered in the stalls and Greg started to speak. 'Well done last night, it was a very good show that went like clockwork, and was about as interesting as… clockwork'. Aha! Harsh words you might think but what followed was a very constructive and much-needed notes session. When a play runs for a long time – in our case since last May – there's always a danger that things will settle, the actors become too comfortable and 'nest' in their favourite bits, forgetting the emotional truth of the moment. The major note for me was that I was 'too noisy', and whilst full of sound and fury at my daughter Hermia's defiance at the beginning of the play, I managed to signify nothing of Egeus's hurt and pain, which is essential if he is to be more than a psychotically splenetic cipher. Greg's theme for us all was to remember the emotional journey of the play and not to take any point in the narrative for granted. He often speaks of the 'crossroads' that exist for a character in a play, moments where the story could turn left, right or go straight on, when an important decision made in the moment on stage to follow a particular path needs to be fully invested in and not just driven straight over. For instance when near the end of the play Theseus the duke asks Egeus:

> *But speak, Egeus; is not this the day*
> *That Hermia should give answer of her choice?*

his reply:

It is, my lord.

should not be taken for granted. Given the harsh
punishment that faces Hermia if she defies him – death
or enforced nunhood – it's better to play the possibility
that he could change his mind and take a different
direction, instead of sticking to his guns and steaming
straight ahead.

Greg's notes were taken on the chin and the second
preview had a fresher feel to it. In his customary
preview/press night tannoy communications he seemed
very pleased with the performance and paid tribute
to the ease with which we'd executed his notes. It
struck me that we could do this because we'd lived and
breathed these plays for 11 months, and our shared
experience together had borne incredible mutual trust;
testament to what a strong group 'The Blues' really are.

T HERE were no notes today. Indeed Greg was to
leave us for a while as he had to go to South Africa
for the opening of an RSC co-production with Baxter
Theatre Centre of *The Tempest* that will be coming to
The Courtyard in February, with Tony Sher as Prospero.
But we *did* have a matinee, which was a bit of a shock
to the system as *Hamlet* only played six shows a week so
it'd been months since we'd done two shows in one day.

The previews have been well received and with only
a couple of technical glitches we're looking forward to
next week's press night.

Week commencing
Monday 19th January

WE had one last preview on Monday and press night on Tuesday, after which we all crammed into the front-of-house bars for our final press night party.

No rest for the wicked, for it was understudy rehearsals Wednesday afternoon for the run the following week, a matinee Thursday, more rehearsals Friday and a matinee Saturday.

The Next Week...

OUR path to the final understudy run was eased by our collective familiarity with the routine, the kind of ease borne of working together for nearly a year and an endorsement of the ensemble principle. The understudy tech was Tuesday and the run itself was followed inexorably by tea and cake on Wednesday. All went without a hitch; we've clicked along so well as a company and it's a shame that soon we will be compelled to go our separate ways.

So goodnight unto you all ...

THE understudy run was done and dusted, the sun well and truly setting and shadows lengthening inexorably over our wonderful season. At this stage of proceedings people are either planning holidays, chasing work, or are lucky enough to already *have* work for when we finish; as far as I know the latter applies to two of our number thus far. I've gone up for a couple of things, a film and a theatre job, but have heard nothing certain yet, so I've been compelled to dip my toe into the chilly waters of tempworld again, re-establishing contacts in London and trying to forge new ones in the West Midlands. I only hope that in these recession-hit times there will be work of some kind to be had.

ALTHOUGH all official RSC rehearsals are over, our enterprising Assistant Director Cressida has been rehearsing a version of Tom Stoppard's *Rosencrantz and Guildenstern are Dead*, with Sam Alexander and Tom Davey reprising the roles they played in *Hamlet*. They've been rehearsing for some weeks, snatching time whenever they could within our busy schedule. Today was the premiere of the production, with another planned for Monday. Cress asked me to record it on Rod Smith's video camera – he played the Player King and Ryan Gage the boy Alfred. It was staged as a circumambulation of the entire Novello. A small invited audience met in the foyer including Penny and Oliver, and it was lovely to see them again. However, mid-chat our amiable milling

Friday 30th January

about was rudely interrupted when Cress, following the understudy run and her triumphant *Hamlet,* and thus with her acting career now fully established, burst into the space playing a somewhat neurotically forceful usher and corralled us all upstairs into one of the bars for the start of the play. From there we as the audience followed the action, led – nay dragged and cajoled – by Cress's hilarious usher, weaving our way back to the foyer for another scene, then through the back of the circle where on the distant stage Ed Bennett was reciting 'To be or not to be…', into another bar then finally for the play's conclusion on to the Novello stage itself. It was a brilliantly witty, site-specific re-working of Stoppard's play and Cress is hoping to produce it elsewhere after we've finished, to which end she's invited quite a few industry bods to the Monday showing. I hope that I captured enough of it on video for it to be entertaining for us and maybe useful in securing a future life for it.

**Saturday
31st January**

TWO shows today and our penultimate week complete. I didn't go home this weekend but stayed up in London as it's Philip's birthday and our other housemate David had organised a surprise party for him on Sunday. Unfortunately Zoë had to go back to Alcester to look after Milly and sort out dog-sitters for the following week, as Zoë's mum was unable to look after her. The party was a huge success and it was great to see friends I hadn't seen for years. David had prepared some beautiful food and there were fireworks in the garden, all the more magical as it had started to snow…

I WOKE up to see the garden transformed into a winter wonderland, and to hear via the *Today* programme that the country was paralysed. I phoned Zoë who was at home in Warwickshire and unsurprisingly she was unable to get to work in London. Later in the morning I got a call from Katie Vine, our company manager, who was stuck at home in Manchester. She told me that Monday's show was in the balance. As it transpired the call came later confirming that the show wasn't to go on and I had an unexpected night off. Since there was little point in attempting to go out I set about consuming the party leftovers, played my guitar and watched television.

Monday 2nd February

B USINESS as usual and we were back on. I learned that had we attempted a show last night there'd've been no sound and no stage management, as all of them were stranded in various parts of the South East. A further unfortunate consequence of the weather was that the Monday showing of *Ros and Guil* had been cancelled which was gutting for all concerned, *but* I believe it's been rescheduled for the beginning of March.

3rd February

4th February

A GOOD show and The President was in! That is, The President of the RSC, and heir to the throne, Prince Charles. He came to the stage afterwards to congratulate us all as we stood in a horseshoe shape to shake his hand. The innate confidence with which royalty deport themselves is always fascinating to behold; I like to observe closely in case I'm called upon to play a monarch one day.

5th February

WHAT is it with the lovers waking scene in the second half? First you may remember the unfortunate flatulent lady in the front row of The Courtyard who made it very difficult for us not to dissolve into howls of laughter a few months ago. On another occasion in the summer, half-way though the scene I suddenly realised that I'd forgotten to put my Egeus moustache back on, causing me to break out into a cold sweat, hoping that no-one had noticed that the stuffy patriarch had apparently had a bit of a makeover. Tonight as I was stomping moodily across the stage I noticed, alas too late as I trod upon it, a large piece of gaffer tape on the stage that attached itself to my shoe. If I tried to move it flapped about and made a loud ripping noise as it was pulled off the stage whenever I lifted my foot to walk. Vainly I performed an elaborate ballet in an attempt to remove it with my other foot, but had to spend almost the entire scene rooted to the spot; trés amusant for Ed and Tom and me, but at least they can to look happy at that point!

The final week ticked down, we received our final pay packets on Thursday and there was a move to go for a drink together with crew and stage management, since whatever party arrangements we might have for Saturday they'll be dismantling the set and packing up the props. Friday came and went and then it was our very last day.

◼

I HURTLED down Camden Road on my bike for the last time. I got my very last early lunch from the Italian café opposite, delicious homemade pesto pasta. At the half we had our very last warm-up for 'Philomel' in the bowels of the earth with Julian. The matinee came and went and for my evening meal I opted for curry from the takeaway in Covent Garden market as my last supper. Over the weeks I'd lived on takeaways for either an early lunch and/or supper to eat at the theatre as there's no green room canteen like at The Courtyard. Japanese, Italian, Indian, Chinese had been consumed in rotation and delicious as they were – mostly – I can't say I'll miss them. I'm looking forward to cooking in my own kitchen again. The Rugby Six Nations championship was on in the green room, watched with varying degrees of interest by cast and crew who drank tea, ate, came and went about their final duties in the matinee/evening interregnum.

Saturday 7th Feb

The last beginners was called and down the million stairs I went. There were the customary best wishes for a final night, and Greg was back from South Africa. I always try to go into a hyper-normal mode on last nights – especially *very* last nights – so as not to fall into the trap of squeezing every last bit of value out of my favourite bits and distorting the story. The audience may or may not be aware that our journey finishes here, but we should give them *The Dream* untrammelled with our own feelings about the end of the run. It was a fine last performance, the final rendition of Paul Englishby's beautiful setting of Glimmering Light was sung, and Mark Hadfield stepped forward to end the play for the last time.

> *If we shadows have offended*
> *Think but this and all is mended …*
> *… Else the Puck a liar call;*
> *So, good night unto you all.*
> *Give me your hands, if we be friends,*
> *And Robin shall restore amends.*

Blackout, fin de comédie…

The audience response was terrific, and as I ran forward to take my bow I wondered, as I always do, when and where I'd do my next play, or indeed if I'd ever work again. Such was the applause a final extra bow was taken, and we were done: off stage, into the corridors and up the stairs, passing the crew who were already hovering like vultures ready to start ripping everything down.

The RSC had laid on some champagne in the front-of-house bar. We gathered and celebrated our year together for the very last time – always a little low-key these occasions. Greg gave a speech, saying how proud he was of us all and to thanking us for our hard work. Then we went on to our last night party proper in a club in Adams Street. As I was waiting at the bar, to my surprise and delight I heard the unmistakably sonorous tones of Patrick Stewart, who had been to see *Oliver* at Drury Lane (our theatre next door neighbours) and had come to meet us to say au revoir, as had Susie Sainsbury, Deputy Chairman of the Board. It was a lovely evening. I wanted to be up and away off home early in the morning but stayed longer than planned; who knows when my next last night would be, I wanted to make the most of this one. Finally, reluctantly, I said my goodbyes to friends and colleagues in the hope that our paths will cross again, and rode carefully back up the hill to Islington. Time to reflect...

For the last few months I've been working for one of the most important companies of its kind on earth. It has a massive, global profile, the work it does is sought by thousands the world over; today my job there ended and I'm sad. Fond farewells have been said and good luck wishes exchanged with people I've grown to love and have had a fantastic time with. As I left The Novello for the last time I repeated that rhetorical question addressed to self by so many actors, repeated mantra-like ad nauseum, whenever a job finishes: 'When will I be back? Will I ever be back? Will I ever work like this ever again?' The ambiguous answer to this is always '...maybe never...maybe never! This terrible prospect chills my soul and I grimace involuntarily. 'Nonsense, you most probably will' reassures the angel on my right shoulder, instantly reminding me of the inevitable cycle of an actor's life. Who knows when or in what capacity I'll be plying my trade next? That's the actor's lot. There's no set path, our territory is a jungle and we must be stoic about the unpredictability of our fate and try not take it personally, being prepared to make our own luck and grab whatever opportunities may come along with both hands. I'm minded of Hamlet's lines to Horatio:

If it be now, 'tis not to come; if it be not to come, it will be now; if it be not now, yet it will come: the readiness is all...

I was on the road the next day by 10:45 and back home in Alcester by lunchtime.

Epilogue

I T'S five o'clock, the champagne glasses are full. Zoë, my mum and dad and I are all looking forward to the first transmission of the television version of *Hamlet*. It's funny how this job has reverberated through the year. There were rumours that a television version might happen during the London season; indeed I'd've been AMAZED if the RSC hadn't attempted to make such a thing happen. In fact towards the end of the run availability checks had been made for possible shooting in June, but then the season had ended with nothing more being said. I had tried to forget about the possibility.

After finishing in London, within the parameters of allowing myself a couple of weeks of leisure, I chased acting work and signed on with a couple of temp agencies, keeping active in an attempt not to slide into a post-RSC slough of despond. I was, for a time, very pleased to be back in the real world again. I cooked some great food in my own kitchen, enjoyed home life and free evenings. In fact in the first week of unemployment I got an audition for a well-known TV series. Result! The meeting was on Friday the 13th as it happened; I tripped down to London and got the job, and really looked forward to doing it, delighted to've been lucky enough to land something so soon after the RSC. Hmmm... I seem to remember joshing to myself about the fact that the audition was on Friday 13th and that it was lucky I wasn't superstitious. Well, I got a call from my agent a couple of weeks later and the producers of this VERY well known and popular TV series had decided they didn't want me after all as they'd realised they could use one of their semi-regular actors. My guess was that this was the cheaper option, and that no doubt they were driven by fears of the deep recession that gripped the country. Much as I understood the fiscal rationale, I was FURIOUS at this

dishonourable and cynical decision. Anyway, life goes
on and I got temporary work as Administrator to the
Quality Engineers department at Halfords head office
in Redditch: back to spreadsheets and stationery.

A couple of little acting jobs came up in the
intervening weeks: a voice-over and some work for the
RSC, which I was able to fit in with my Halfords career.
Being local I'm often asked to do these workshop-type
things, which are usually very interesting and at least
keep the juices flowing. Zoë returned home at the end
of March to put As You Like it into The Courtyard having
finally finished the long three-month rehearsal process
with the new ensemble. Having done that she started
a new and exciting RSC adventure turning away from
stage management having got a new job as an assistant
producer working for Denise Wood.

Then in mid-April, Illuminations Media, who were
behind the idea to do the ill-fated live broadcast at the
end of Stratford, contacted my agent and confirmed
that a film version in cahoots with the BBC was
definitely going ahead. Even better, they'd managed to
get everyone from the original cast. BRILLIANT! I held
my breath until all was signed, sealed and delivered,
my normal out-of-work-actor paranoia exacerbated
by my disappointment earlier in the year, reminding
myself of that old adage 'many a slip 'twixt cup and lip'.
However, finally the contract arrived at which point I
was absolutely confident that all was well. We were to
start on the 1st June, I couldn't wait!

1st June and YAY!!! It was good to be back at the
newly-refurbed rehearsal rooms in Clapham. They've
moved the entrance to one side of the building, there's
a lift, the green room's poshed up and there's even a
computer room. The rehearsal rooms still have the
same shabby charm, which I love. It was wonderful
to see my old Blue Company chums again – well, not

quite everyone because Patrick was up to his eyes in the existential conundrum that is *Waiting for Godot* in the West End. He couldn't join us, which meant that I was Claudius/Ghost for the day. As we all excitedly caught up with one another following the four-month interregnum since London, it became clear that getting all of us back together again had been a logistical challenge, bravely faced down and brilliantly solved. Apart from Patrick's commitment, Minnie Gale was in *As You Like It* in Stratford, Oliver Ford Davies in *All's Well That Ends Well* at The National, Ryan Gage on a nationwide tour with *Quadrophenia* and Riann Steele in *Holby City*. On the other hand David had just finished *Dr Who* – literally the week before – and was now free as a bird!

John Wyver and Seb Grant of Illuminations, who were clearly as excited as we were at the prospect of capturing this very special production on film, talked us through what the next three weeks held for us. We were on a very tight schedule with three hours of film to shoot in just three weeks, averaging about 10 minutes a day; the norm is a fraction of this. Seb and John also talked about the location chosen to film *Hamlet* – this was St Joseph's College, a derelict Roman Catholic seminary built in the 19th century in North London – and we were sworn to secrecy as to its whereabouts for obvious reasons (although I'd already checked it out online at work and already told a few people … oops!).

The plan for the morning was to take the dustsheets off the play, shake them thoroughly, throw them to one side and do a sort of free run-through, recalling the emotional landscapes of our work from six months ago but forgetting the physical terrain of The Courtyard stage. This project was not to be a simple film record of what we'd finished six months earlier, nor would it be a blockbuster movie version with huge sets and grandiose cliff-top vistas. Greg explained that to preserve a sense of the theatricality of the original we would be occupying a world of 'vivid neutrality', one in which Elsinore would be defined by Shakespeare's words, the atmospheric spaces of the chosen location and the manner in which they would be shot and lit. The dominating feature of the stage version was the mirrored back wall that gave a sense of the action being watched from all sides, heightening the sense of surveillance and paranoia in the Danish court and also reflecting the audience back at themselves – the watchers being watched. To give this same feeling for the TV version Greg had the idea of including CCTV footage that would at given moments be cut in to the normal mode of shooting, thus adding a similar meta-observational dimension.

After plans were discussed we were up on our feet. In order to erase the well-trod paths that mapped out the spatial life of the stage production we formed a large circle of chairs and ran through the play from beginning to end, entering and exiting each scene from where we sat and improvising where to move as we went. I had great fun standing in for Patrick as Claudius and was thrilled at the opportunity of being the channel for this great doubling of parts one more time. Considering we hadn't done the play since 10th January there were remarkably few cobwebs to be brushed away. Everyone clicked right back into the groove that had been forged between us over a year of working together. In the afternoon we went through the fights and then it simply would've been churlish not to go for a reunion pint.

The next morning I set off in the early morning sun. I was staying with Philip again in North London so my drive to Mill Hill was a relatively short one. As I neared my destination, a short way up the A1, I could see St

Joseph's towering redbrick spire mounted by a giant statue of the saint. I remembered that many years ago, when I used to go to cricket practice in Barnet, I always wondered what this extraordinary looking building was. Well, now I know.

I turned into the drive, declared myself to the security guard, and wound my way uphill to the massive college complex, past the generators that would provide power for lights, cameras, action etc. Parking up, I paused for a moment to take in the view over London from this lofty vantage point, then excitedly spun on my heel to find out what was afoot. The site was a beehive of activity, a bustle of crew carrying cables and cases of kit in and out of the entrance to the building and walkie-talkies crackling sharply in the morning air. I walked past make-up and was ushered by Jennie Fava, the 2nd Assistant Director, up past the location bus and catering van, to a street of caravans either side of a wide, tree-sheltered path where my dressing room for the day was. Site-specific locations such as this become temporary mini-towns. On this very first day of filming we shot the battlement scenes in the morning, in which Hamlet sees the ghost for the first time with Horatio and Marcellus. To preserve his energy Patrick wasn't called early, so Sam Alexander had kindly agreed to be his stand-in to set up the shots (he had been one of the decoy ghosts in the first scene at The Courtyard). What with his bald wig, beard and all I thought he bore an uncanny resemblance to Charles Darwin, though by the end of what was a very hot day he looked more like a boiled egg with a face drawn on it. Having had breakfast (location food is legendary – an army marches on its stomach after all) I was reunited with Marcellus' military apparell and made my way down Location High Street into the centre of operations. Through the doors, out of sunshine into darkness past glowing screens, lights and cables to the set.

The battlement scenes were to be shot in the cloisters around the central quad of the seminary. We met Toni Staples the 1st Assistant Director who was responsible for the smooth running of the shoot, and were introduced to Chris Seager the Lighting Cameraman who is an absolute genius. The windows had been blacked out, so that only thin slivers of light carved through the smoke that had been pumped into the space and reflected off the wetted floor.

For the first part of the morning Peter, David and I played off Sam's admirable body doubling, then Patrick arrived later for us to complete the angles where his face was visible that we hadn't been able to do earlier. I found it surprisingly liberating to remould Marcellus for TV, bringing the levels down and letting the camera do the work, the dark, dilapidated fabric of this old building contributing to the edginess, fear and uncertainty that drives the narrative of the scene. In the afternoon the dialogue between Young and Old Hamlet was shot. For this the action moved from the cloisters to the nave of the chapel of the college. This space was the main one used for the entire shoot. To render it a blank canvas that could be dressed and adapted for each scene, under Rob Jones' supervision, its interior had been painted black and the columns covered in a dark grey and black marbled sticky-backed plastic. Thus the vivid architectural forms of the building were retained whilst their Victorian gothic specificity subdued.

Late afternoon and Peter and I were called to the chapel to meet Hamlet post-ghost. We caught the last bit of David and Patrick's scene on the monitor, which looked and sounded fantastic. Ours was the final scene in the can. We hadn't managed to get to the very top of the play as planned, so poor Rob Curtis had hung about all day for nothing. We would catch up tomorrow.

Having been official RSC blogger for the last year I've now been asked to be a Twitterer (Tweeter?) posting live 140-character long news-bites for the shoot from the set along with Tom Davey and Sam Alexander. I've also been asked to help judge a competition devised by John Wyver for the best summary of the plot of *Hamlet* expressed in 140 characters! I couldn't help but notice that a sonnet is 14 lines long, with five feet and 10 syllables per line; a simple calculation thus reveals that the number of syllables in a sonnet is the same as the number of characters in a tweet. It should therefore be possible to define the DNA of a sonnet by, say, the first character of each syllable. Unfortunately no one was sufficiently impressed by my observation to explore the idea further... can't think why.

The next day (Wednesday 3rd June) started as before with David solus filming the first soliloquy:

'Oh that this too, too solid flesh...'

Ewen, Peter and I were called a little later for the end of Act 1 Scene 2 when Barnado, Marcellus and Horatio tell Hamlet what they've seen on the battlements. Overnight the nave had been transformed from a purgatorial black box to the throne room of Elsinore castle, with gilt-framed mirrors, furniture, and the original chandeliers from The Courtyard. After another spectacular location lunch it was back to the battlements and indeed back in time, to the very beginning of the play.

That evening it was back to Warwickshire for me for a few days, and back to office work. In my absence the filming continued apace, on amongst other things the big opening court scene, the closet scene, the nunnery scene and Laertes' departure. I, meanwhile, sweated over spreadsheets and reports and couldn't wait to return.

I was back on Tuesday the 9th June for a full English location breakfast and the final scene. There was an added complication today as there was a London Tube strike. It didn't affect me much as I was driving, although to allow for extra traffic I got up at 6:00 and left a little earlier. As most of the cast were called today I've lost exclusive use of my trailer, and there are four of us crammed into the same space. For the first part of the morning it was *my* turn to be Patrick's body-double… I hoped that Sam wasn't too bitter about losing the role to me, but hey-ho that's showbiz dahhling! Standing in for Patrick was necessary not only to line up the shots but also as an eye-line for the other actors to use for their close-ups – better me than empty space (at least I hope so!). On Patrick's arrival I schizophrenically morphed into Marcellus again… and then became Claudius again when Patrick had to leave for his evening show at about 5:00. Ryan Gage (Osric) had to leave at tea-time to be driven to Bath for *his* evening show.

A day off, then back again on Thursday the 11th for Ophelia's funeral, which was filmed outside in the quad. A real grave had been dug for Minnie to be lowered into, which was really rather creepy. The first part of the scene was filmed the day before – the dialogue between the two gravediggers and of course Yorick. André Tchaikowsky had followed up on his theatrical career and established himself as a fine screen actor. The weather had been pretty dire yesterday and we prayed it would hold out today, and it did in an unexpectedly unwelcome way. Because the day before had been rainy and cloudy, when the sun shone today it cast shadows that would be inconsistent with what was already in the

can. At one point Chris Seager had to realign a scene
so that it could be shot in the shadow of St Joseph's
spire. Then it got so silly that Greg decided it'd be better
use of our ever-diminishing time to rehearse the play
scene indoors in advance of shooting it the next day.
Eventually we managed to get everything done, and as
I left John handed me a printout of the tweets entered
into our plot summary competition over the last few
days for me to peruse.

Friday the 12th and it was play day... but first things
first. Over yet another stupendous breakfast John and I
picked six of the best *Hamlet* plot tweets.

Back in the chapel we set up and shot the arrival
of the court and the dumb show. Unfortunately we
couldn't fly David Ajala in and Sam Dutton out so it was
all done with camera angles and the expert eye of Chris
Seager. Today, however, there was another cameraman
on set – David Tennant. He was issued with a small
hand-held camera to film Patrick's reactions to *The
Mousetrap*, thus unkennelling the king's occulted guilt.
In fact he was issued with two: one for when he was in
the scene off-camera, with which he actually took shots
that would be used in the finished film, and one when
he was in shot which was a little super 8 type in keeping
with the late 20th-century design concept. The idea was
that the footage taken with the real camera would be
processed post-production to look like a home movie,
Hamlet having carried out his own surveillance in order
to try to determine what his course of action should be.

Lunch, and then on to the sumptuously-costumed
high-Elizabethan *Murder of Gonzago*. For some reason
there was quite a bit of hanging around today, so while
the various set ups were being done, games of bat and
ball and football were played in the sun by the make-
up wagon. I was Patrick at the beginning and end of
today. In the morning predominantly for sightlines and

blocking and in the late afternoon I physically stood in for him out of shot for the actual filming of the end of the scene. I therefore felt more of a responsibility than just being an eye-line, as I had to give something for David to play off for his close up. I had also done this the other day when we filmed the very end of the play, when Hamlet forces Claudius to drink from the poison cup.

Saturday the 13th I was called late afternoon to be a soldier in Fortinbras' army on the way to the little patch of ground. There were about eight of us, marching along the edge of a shot taken from on high as if from Fortinbras' helicopter, so that just the tops of our heads and shoulders and rucksacks were visible, rendering us a necessary anonymity. We marched into shot then ran round to enter again to give the illusion of the 20,000 men, with the encounter between Rod Smith as The Captain and Hamlet in the middle.

I returned for my final two days on Wednesday 17th June. Today we were to shoot what was affectionately known as the Keystone Cops chase sequence after Hamlet has killed Polonius. As we sat down to breakfast Greg walked up the hill past the location bus and we breakfasters to talk to John. They both looked very serious and it transpired that overnight the main camera had been stolen along with some lenses and other items of equipment. It goes without saying that this was quite a blow, and very odd – St Joe's is a huge labyrinthine complex and there was supposed to be 24-hour security. Quite naturally there was a collective sense of outrage, and in any spare moment through the day I found myself quite involuntarily wandering around the periphery of St Joseph's in the vain hope of spotting some clue, or indeed the camera itself discarded under a bush or in one of the many out-buildings which looked like they were originally built for keeping livestock. The stolen camera had been a state-of-the-art Red camera, and apparently there were only about 100 in the whole country, so how the thief was planning to sell this on was a mystery to all of us. Luckily there was a spare camera, and even more crucially the rushes from the previous day had been safely stowed off site.

We filmed the chase sequence around the cloisters that had served as the battlements, then the end of the chase with the antic prince finally captured on the stairs in a stairwell. Rehearsing in situ before shooting, on being cornered, David instinctively leapt onto the banisters and played the scene swinging around the newel, which was very exciting! Unfortunately too exciting from a health and safety point of view. Ah well, I suppose they might've had a point: the leading actor of an eagerly anticipated television film, swinging out over a 20-foot drop with only three weeks to shoot? Fair enough!

On the previous Saturday there'd apparently been a spontaneous reunion of The Captain of the Fairy Band on Dressing Room Street in my absence. Well, today we had another jam in the sun, revisiting some of the old glories and some new ones, working out chords or downloading them from the internet on the location office computer. John Wyver let loose with a superb rendition of 'Brown Eyed Girl' by Van Morrison.

Thursday the 18th was my last day, my last location breakfast, midmorning coffee, lunch, tea and cake. This had been designated as the 'pick up' day. That is the day where anything that we haven't managed to get in the can on schedule is shot. Among the pick ups was the end of Act One Scene One, so we reel back in time to end at the beginning again, ghost-busting on the battlements. I bade a final farewell to Marcellus, my old friends and the new ones I'd got to know all too briefly on the shoot. Filming went on until the 23rd June after which there was a wrap party, which unfortunately I couldn't go to.

Four months later many of us were reunited for the cast and crew screening at The Soho Hotel. It was a fantastic evening, drinks before, then into the screening room. I couldn't get over how HUGE I looked in my scenes; it is well known that on a TV screen one appears much fatter than in real life and to my eye I seemed to be the size of a HOUSE. Once I'd got over myself, and my own vanity, I thoroughly enjoyed this very special film and couldn't wait to see it on the small screen...

And that's where I am now, on the brink of a new year, a new decade. We settle down, the screen fades to black, sound of wind and boot on stone floor, a soldier is revealed walking alone around the battlements at night captured in the chilly grainy monochrome of CCTV. He's frightened and cold and as he turns a corner a voice cries out from the darkness... 'Who's there?'

PHOTOGRAPHS

Key to photographers

ALL PHOTOGRAPHS BY ELLIE KURTTZ © RSC EXCEPT:

EK*: ELLIE KURTTZ © RSC/ILLUMINATIONS MEDIA

CB: CRESSIDA BROWN

GB: GIGI BUFFINGTON

RC: ROBERT CURTIS

SK: STEVE KEELEY

KO: KEITH OSBORN

Opposite:

Top; the Athenian courtiers and mechanicals dance the chorus-line finale to the Bergomask [EK]

Middle left: Greg Doran talks to Joe Dixon (Bottom) clad in his asses head, it should also be noted that Joe is wearing padding [EK]

Middle right: the fairy band rehearse with their doll puppets, rescued from obscurity in Greg's parents' loft [EK]

Bottom: Puck (Mark Hadfield) tells Oberon (Peter De Jersey) how he has successfully (he thinks) completed his mission [EK]

Above: Lysander (Tom Davey) held aloft as we fairies (Self, David Ajala, Rob Curtis) take control of his mind and body [EK]

Above: Bunraku puppetry to the fore from Sam Dutton, Minnie Gale and Riann Steele while Titania (Andrea Harris) tells the story of the Changeling Boy [EK]

Above: A moustachioed Egeus (Self) brandishes the offending 'sweetmeat' given to Hermia by Lysander, the other love tokens lie scattered on the stage [EK]

Above: Quince (Rod Smith) delivers the Pyramus and Thisbe Prologue á la Grotowski introducing Thisbe (Ryan Gage), Wall (Ricky Champ) and Pyramus (Joe Dixon) [EK]

Above: Hermia (Kathryn Drysdale) wakes from her nightmare to the curiosity and amusement of us fairies (Rob Curtis, Riann Steele, David Ajala, Sam Dutton, Self, Minnie Gale, Sam Alexander and Zoë Thorne) [EK]

Above: Reconciled, Oberon and Titania take flight as dawn breaks and Bottom slumbers on below [EK]

Above: Greg Doran contemplates the skull of Andre Tchaikowsky who played Yorick [EK]

Above: Polonius (Oliver Ford-Davies) ponders the nature of madness during our first run of Hamlet [EK]

Above: Tea break and chats in the rehearsal room between Patrick Stewart and Penny Downie, David Tennant and Jim Hooper [EK]

Above: 'The Circle' and our first non-stop read, straight through the play [EK]

Above Left: Claudius (Patrick Stewart) thinks on his feet at the news of Hamlet's unexpected return [EK] and *Above Right*: Hamlet (David Tennant) contemplates Yorick's and all of our fates, during the first run-through [EK]

Top: we learn some drill with Sgts 'Robbo' Robertson and Nick Casswell from the local TA [EK]

Above Left: Lynn Darnley (Left) and Gigi Buffington do some voice work with the company [EK]

Above: Barnado and Marcellus (Ewen Cummins, Self) try to restrain Hamlet as the duel with Laertes gets out of control [EK]

Above: Paul Englishby takes a singing session as we all get a flavour of Elizabethan folks songs which he based Ophelia's songs on [EK]

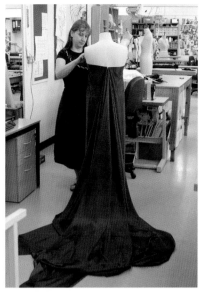

Above: elements of the set, the chandeliers and Gertrude's costume being made at Timothy's Bridge Road workshop [EK]

Below: the finished articles in situ [EK]

Above: Marcellus and Horatio (Peter De J) cower in the gloom following the ghost's exhortation to swear Hamlet's oath [EK]

Above: Feverish exultation following the Murder of Gonzago and apparent unmasking of the king's guilt [EK]

Above: Minnie Gale being made up for Ophelia's 'mad scene' mid-show by Kim Boyce and Rachel Seal surrounded by the paraphernalia of the wig room [CB]

Right: *And will 'a not come again?*
 No, no he is dead,
 Go to thy death-bed
 He never will come again. [EK]

Above: having been Laertes' noisy rabble at the back of the auditorium, already in our costumes for the Norwegian army, we make our way thro' the foyer to backstage to gain a little patch of ground for the 'eggshell' scene [CB]

Right: Sweets to the sweet; farewell!
I hop'd thou shouldst have been my
Hamlet's wife;
I thought thy bride bed to have deck'd
sweet maid,
And not have strew'd thy grave [EK]

Below: First and Second gravedigger (Mark Hadfield and a heavily bewigged and bespotted Sam Alexander) just before Hamlet and Horatio enter [EK]

Above: in the first week of rehearsals David and Ed slowly and methodically start to work on the big fight at the end of the play with Terry King [EK]

Below: The fight realised in action in situ [EK]

Below: an archery lesson for the Princes of France and her entourage [CB]

Above: having been sung to in the traditional manner Oliver blows out the candles on his birthday cake! [CB]

Above: Matt Aston, David and Kev Wimperis just before Matt and Kev left for New York to run the marathon [SK]

Below: Self and Jim in front of the old RST being demolished [RC]

Above: Me finding my inner Marcade in rehearsal [EK]

Below: John Blizard now a retired dresser, aged about 18 months, in front of the old RST being built [Probably taken circa 1931 by his mother]

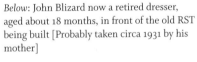

Above: Berowne (David T) comes between Costard (Ricky Champ) and Armado (Joe Dixon) as they fight over Jaquenetta (Riann Steele) [EK]

Below: Hercules (Zoë Thorne as Moth) fights the snake in *The Nine Worthies* [EK]

Below: Andrea sings 'Play that Funky Music' in the greatest gig in the world, Self on fretless bass [GB]

Above: the bitter-sweet end of the play, Rosaline (Nina Sosanya) makes Berowne swear to turn his wit to helping the speechless sick for a twelvemonth before she will marry him [EK]

Below: virtuosically accompanying himself on his ukulele, Dumaine (Sam Alexander) sings of his love for Maria, spied on by King Ferdinand (Ed Bennett), Berowne (David) and Longaville (Tom Davey) [EK]

Above: We mummers of Navarre perform a clog dance having sung bawdy songs to the audience at the end of the interval to open the 2nd half of the show. At the front is Rob Curtis, Sam D and David A, I'm back right with the green face [EK]

Below Left: Maria (Natalie Walter) and Katherine (Kathryn Drysdale) in full Elizabethan splendour, [EK]

Below Right: Marcade (Self) mars Arcadia with news of the Princess' fathers death [EK]

Above: Greg and David on set [EK*]

Below left: Penny and Ed prepare for the graveyard scene while Chris Seager sets up the shot [KO]

Below Top Right: Ellie Kurttz in action on location [KO]

Below Bottom Right: an impromptu jam on location as we relive the glory of The Captain of Our Fairy Band days [RC]

Left: The happy cast and crew near the end of our wonderful journey together [EK*]

THE PLOTS OF THE PLAYS

The plots of the plays

A Midsummer Night's Dream

IT is four nights before the nuptial hour of Theseus, Duke of Athens, and Hyppolyta, Queen of the Amazons. Their eager anticipation of pomp, triumph and revelling is punctured by the arrival of Egeus and his daughter Hermia with two young Athenian gentlemen, Lysander and Demetrius in train. Egeus wants Hermia to marry Demetrius who proclaims his love for her, but to Egeus's rage, she is in love with Lysander who he doesn't approve of at all. To enforce his will Egeus calls on the Duke to invoke an ancient Athenian law which dictates that if Hermia disobeys him she must be put to death or spend the rest of her life in a convent; Theseus has no choice but to advise Hermia of her options. Consequently Lysander and Hermia resolve to elope and arrange to meet in the wood a league outside Athens and then make their way to his dowager aunt, who lives seven leagues away, where they can be wed. They tell their friend Helena of this scheme, but as she is in love with Demetrius (who incidentally is rumoured to have already had some type of tryst with her) she hatches a plan to tell him where Hermia is off to so that she can then follow him into the wood to try to win him over.

Meanwhile a group of Athenian tradesmen have been short-listed to perform the tragedy of *Pyramus and Thisbe* before Theseus and Hyppolyta on their wedding day and decide that it'd be most expedient to rehearse in the wood a mile without the town (see above) to prepare for this dream gig.

In the wood outside Athens in the world of the fairies there is a bitter row between Oberon and Titania, the king and queen of that realm, over the custody an Indian 'Changeling' boy who Titania has care of following the death of his natural mother in giving birth to him. Oberon demands that Titania hand over the boy but she defies him.

Furious at Titania's refusal Oberon sends his servant Puck to find the flower love-in-idleness from which he can distil a potion which, when applied to Titania's eyes when she's sleeping, will make her fall passionately in love with the first creature she sees when she awakes. While Puck is on his mission Oberon sees Helena in pursuit of Demetrius, who has indeed left Athens in pursuit of Hermia. Touched by Helena's plight at Demetrius's savage rejection of her, on Puck's return he orders him to put some juice on Demetrius' eyes so that Helena's love for him can be requited. Puck goes off in search of this disdainful youth in Athenian garments.

Lysander and Hermia are completely lost in the wood and resolve to sleep and tarry for the comfort of the day. When they've dropped off Puck enters and finds them, assumes that Lysander is Demetrius and applies the potion to *his* eyes, which would've been fine except that Helena enters and stumbles across the slumbering Lysander waking him up, upon which he falls in love with her instantly and sets off in pursuit leaving Hermia asleep and alone; she wakes soon after Lysander's desertion, puzzled and frightened she goes in search of her beloved.

The Mechanicals start to rehearse their play in the wood as planned, Puck mischievously transforms Bottom's human head to that of an ass and his fellow thesps flee in terror. It so happens the spot they've chosen is very near to where Titania is sleeping. Oberon has exacted his revenge and doused her eyes with the love-in-idleness potion so when she wakes up she falls in love with the ass-headed Bottom, and orders her fairy servants to tend to him and to lead him to the intimate confines of her fairy bower.

Puck reports back to Oberon on how Titania has fallen in love with Bottom and also his success, he thinks, of his mission to find and drug Demetrius with the potion. At this point Demetrius enters having found Hermia and is desperately wooing her. She rebukes him suspecting that he has killed Lysander and exits to continue her

search. Exhausted he gives up the chase to rest and sleep. Oberon realises Puck's error and in an effort to put things right puts the love juice
on Demetrius' eyes. No sooner has he done this when Helena enters
pursued by Lysander and Demetrius wakes up and falls passionately in
love with her. However she thinks that both of them are mocking her
with fake ardour. Then Hermia finds enters and expresses her puzzlement at Lysander's strange behaviour, which Helena takes as evidence
that she too is in on the joke. However Hermia thinks that Helena
has deliberately stolen Lysander's heart and an almighty row ensues at
the end of which Lysander and Demetrius exit cheek by jowl to duel
for Helena's love. Hermia, who appears to have inherited some of her
father's spleen, turns on Helena and chases her off into the wood.

Puck misdirects the four lovers up and down the paths of the wood
and engineers it that they all collapse in exhaustion in the same place
and fall asleep close to each other in their couples; he undoes the spell
on Lysander in order that all will be well again.

Blissfully happy, Titania returns from her fairy bower with Bottom
and her entourage who are sent to get various delicacies for him while
the two lovers fall asleep in each other's arms. Oberon enters and has
managed to persuade Titania, in her drug-addled ecstasy, to give him
the Changeling Boy so undoes the hateful imperfection of her eyes.
She awakes and tells Oberon that she'd dreamt she was enamoured of
an ass, Oberon indicates Bottom still asleep and orders Puck to remove
the ass's head. King and Queen are reunited and resolve to bless the
wedding of Theseus and Hippolyta tomorrow midnight; they leave
Bottom alone and asleep.

Up and out early on the royal wedding morning for a hunting
trip, the Athenian court arrive at the place where Lysander, Hermia,
Demetrius and Helena are sleeping. The young lovers wake and try to
relate what has happened, Egeus interrupts in outrage insisting that
Theseus bring the law upon Lysander's head and marry his daughter to
Demetrius. However Demetrius, having returned to his natural taste

now proclaims his true love for Helena and the Duke overrules Egeus inviting the two young couples to be married with him and Hippolyta later that day.

Bottom wakes and, like Titania, thinks that recent events were but a dream and sets off back to Athens to find the other mechanicals. They are despondent at the loss of their friend and leading man, which also means that their play cannot now go ahead. Bottom's safe return is met with utter delight and they look forward to the real possibility of performing at the palace.

Following the triple wedding Theseus does indeed choose *Pyramus and Thisbe* as the evening's entertainment, which is enjoyed by all … if not entirely for the right reasons. The three couples go to bed and Oberon and Titania bless the palace and their marriages with sweet peace. Puck is left alone on stage to wish the audience goodnight and to invite their applause.

Hamlet

TWO OFFICERS OF the guard at Elsinore castle, Marcellus and Barnado, have seen the ghost of the dead king Hamlet on the battlements and have persuaded Horatio, who is prince Hamlet's best friend and a scholar, to speak to it to find out the reason for its appearance wondering whether it's linked to the fact that Denmark seems to be preparing for war. The ghost appears twice but refuses to answer Horatio's questions; Horatio is convinced that it will speak to young Hamlet and the three resolve to fetch him up to the battlements asap.

Old Hamlet's brother Claudius has succeeded him as king and married his widow Gertrude. Claudius addresses the court acknowledging the moral complexity of the marriage and thanks them for freely going along with it. He further reveals that young Fortinbras of Norway intends to invade Denmark and despatches ambassadors to persuade Fortinbras' uncle to stop him. Next he gives elder states-man Polonius's son Laertes permission to return to France. Lastly he addresses Prince Hamlet who has indicated his intention to return to his studies at Wittenberg University but is persuaded by Gertrude to remain at Elsinore for the time being. The court leaves and Hamlet expresses his despair at his father's death and his mother's marriage to his uncle. Horatio, Marcellus and Barnado enter and tell him what they've seen and after some initial scepticism Hamlet agrees to go with them to the battlements that night and speak to the ghost.

Polonius says goodbye to Laertes and warns his daughter Ophelia off Hamlet's courtship.

In the nipping, eager, cold night air Hamlet, Horatio and Marcellus wait for the ghost. It appears and lures Hamlet away from the other two confirming that it is indeed his father's spirit, telling Hamlet that Claudius had murdered him. Hamlet promises to avenge this crime and when Marcellus and Horatio find him, whilst he doesn't tell them of the murder, he indicates that he will be putting on an antic dispo-sition around the castle and swears them to secrecy about what has happened.

Polonius sends a servant, Reynaldo, to spy on Laertes in France. A distressed Ophelia enters and tells her father that as instructed she has denied Hamlet's access to her but that he has been behaving very strangely, Polonius resolves to tell the king and queen of this.

Two old school friends of Hamlet, Rosencrantz and Guildenstern, have been sent for by Claudius to try and find the cause of Hamlet's apparent affliction. Meanwhile the Danish ambassadors have returned from Norway with mission accomplished as Fortinbras has promised not to invade Denmark. Following this joyful news Polonius expounds the theory that Hamlet's madness is caused by his unrequited love for Ophelia. Hamlet approaches and Claudius dismisses the queen while he and Polonius spy on Hamlet's encounter with Ophelia, who Polonius has brought along in order to loose upon Hamlet to provoke some kind of reaction. Hamlet enters contemplating the nature of being … or not … He spots Ophelia and on imploring her to leave Elsinore and go to a nunnery as a place of virtue he suddenly realises that he's been set up, flies into a rage and storms off. Ophelia is desolate at his state of mind whilst Claudius suspects he isn't actually mad …

Determined to prove he's right Polonius ushers the king and Ophelia away as Hamlet returns. Hamlet plays mad and mocks Polonius who leaves as Rosencrantz and Guildenstern arrive. Hamlet recognises them instantly and very quickly realises that, despite their denials, they've been sent for by the king. It transpires that Rosencrantz and Guildenstern have hired some travelling players for Hamlet's entertainment and bang on cue they arrive. Hamlet greets them warmly and at his request the leading man performs a speech relating the slaughter of Priam by Pyrrhus during the sacking of Troy by the Greeks. Hamlet asks the players to prepare *The Murder of Gonzago* to present to the court, and bids them leave. Now alone, he expresses his frustration with his own inertia thus far, but reveals that he intends to test the veracity of the ghost's accusation by inserting a speech into the play that will prove whether the king is guilty or not.

The king interrogates Rosencrantz and Guildenstern as to what they've found out, which isn't very much, and agrees to attend the players' performance. He confides to Polonius that he intends to send Hamlet away to England.

The court attends the play and at the requisite moment, as the player king is murdered in the manner in which the ghost had described his own, Claudius stops the performance. Hamlet and Horatio (who he has now told of his suspicions) take this as proof of the king's guilt. Polonius returns and tells Hamlet that Gertrude wants a word with him in her closet.

At this turn of events the king orders Rosencrantz and Guildenstern to take Hamlet to England. Alone he then reveals his guilt in a soliloquy after which he kneels to pray for forgiveness. Hamlet enters and is within an ace of exacting his revenge. He stops short because he believes that as Claudius is at prayer that the king will go to heaven so resolves to kill him later; ironically it transpires that Claudius' prayers are but words without any substance.

Polonius has run ahead of Hamlet to tell Gertrude that he's on his way and hides in the closet to listen to what is said. Hamlet arrives and the heat of the exchange between he and his mother is such that Polonius cries for help, Hamlet thinks it is the king and kills him. He then tells Gertrude of Claudius' alleged crime and in a highly-charged exchange between them begs her not to let Claudius sleep with her. In the middle of this the ghost appears and, seen only by Hamlet, tells him not to be so angry with his mother. Hamlet bids goodnight to her and leaves dragging off Polonius' corpse. Claudius arrives and Gertrude tells him what has happened, though not of Hamlet's accusation. The king calls Rosencrantz and Guildenstern and tells them to find Hamlet. Hamlet is brought before the king, tells him where Polonius is and then hears the news of his temporary exile. In a soliloquy Claudius reveals that the correspondence he has sent with Rosencrantz and Guildenstern instructs the English king to execute Hamlet.

Ophelia has gone mad, Laertes returns with a number of followers to avenge Polonius' death for which he blames Claudius. The sight of Ophelia's distraction turns him from his intent, Claudius takes advantage and promises him justice.

Hamlet has jumped ship on his way back to Denmark when he encounters Fortinbras' army marching to occupy a little patch of ground in Poland. He meditates on the human cost of this enterprise and continues on his journey home finally resolved to revenge his father's murder.

Back in Elsinore Claudius is trying to convince Laertes that Hamlet is to blame for Polonius' death. He gets news of Hamlet's imminent return and so hatches a plot to kill Hamlet thus giving Laertes satisfaction and removing the only person who can reveal his guilt. Gertrude enters with the news that Ophelia has drowned.

Hamlet is back and has met Horatio in a graveyard where the burial of a young woman is about to take place. Hamlet exchanges banter with the gravedigger who doesn't realise who he is and shows him the skull of Yorick the court jester who Hamlet knew as a boy, this leads Hamlet to contemplate the transience of human life … The funeral party, the Danish court, arrives and he realises that the grave is for Ophelia. In a state of high dudgeon he makes himself known and publicly declares his love for her. Laertes attacks him and they fight over Ophelia's corpse.

Back at the castle Hamlet tells Horatio how he jumped ship, escaping execution in England and arranged for Rosencrantz and Guildenstern to be killed instead. A courtier, Osric, enters and tells Hamlet that Claudius has requested that Hamlet fence with Laertes; Hamlet agrees. The court arrives, the king's wager and prizes declared and the duel commences. Unexpectedly Hamlet wins the first round and Claudius invites him to drink his health having dropped a poisoned pearl into the wine, apparently as a gift. Hamlet refuses but Gertrude does drink. The duel restarts and gets progressively more violent. In the struggle Laertes cuts Hamlet with his poisoned rapier, Hamlet gets possession of it and wounds Laertes in turn. The queen collapses indicating to Hamlet that the drink is poisoned before she dies. Laertes now dying confesses his part in the plot and tells of the king's guilt before he expires. Hamlet confronts Claudius and wounds him with the poisoned sword then forces him to drink the poison; the king's pleas for help fall on deaf ears and he dies. Hamlet realising that he too is about to shuffle off his mortal coil persuades Horatio not to commit suicide like an antique Roman but to tell his story. Hamlet dies in his friend's arms and Fortinbras enters to take power.

Love's Labour's Lost

KING Ferdinand of Navarre has proclaimed that no women shall be permitted to come within a mile of his court and that he and his three friends Berowne, Dumaine and Longaville will dedicate themselves to study for three years forgoing female company on pain of public shame. The sceptic Berowne points out that the princess of France is expected imminently to do some court business on behalf of her sick and bedrid father. The decree is signed anyway and the four resolve to find entertainment for the duration of their oath through Don Armado, a bombastic Spanish gentleman, and Costard a local swain. No sooner is the ink dry on the pact but Constable Dull arrives with Costard, who Armado has had arrested because he has disobeyed the king's edict by consorting with Jaquenetta, a dairymaid, that it turns out Armado is in love with himself. The king gives Costard over to Armado's custody.

The princess arrives with her three ladies Rosaline, Maria and Katharine and a senior courtier Boyet who she sends to let the king know they've arrived. Boyet returns with the news that the French entourage must set up camp in the field. The king and his three friends come out to meet them and start to fall in love; Berowne with Rosaline, Dumaine with Katherine, Longaville with Maria and the King with the Princess.

Meanwhile Armado tells his page Moth of the depth of his love for Jaquenetta and frees Costard on condition that he deliver a love-letter to her. Berowne then employs him to deliver one to Rosaline. Unfortunately Costard delivers Don Armado's to the princess, who reads it out to the French court.

Enter Sir Nathaniel, a curate, to his partner in pedantry Holofernes, a schoolmaster and Dull who've have been observing the princess and her party on a deer hunt with Dull. Costard has delivered Berowne's sonnet to Jaquenetta who asks Sir Nathaniel to read it to her and Holofernes tells her to deliver it to the king.

In another part of the park Berowne enters despairing at the fact that he's in love with Rosaline. He hides as the King Ferdinand approaches, who likewise is in love with the princess which he expresses by means of a poem. *He* hides as Longaville enters reciting a sonnet for Maria and finally *he* hides when Dumaine arrives reading an ode he has written. Inevitably, each having spied on each other, all their covers are blown but Berowne provides a rationale for them all to give up their vows and woo their beloveds. They decide that it'd be fun to do this by disguising themselves as Russians. Boyet gets wind of this and warns the ladies of their approach. The women then don masks and the boys woo the wrong girls. Realising the hopelessness of the Russian idea they retreat and enter again to be mocked mercilessly by the women.

Meanwhile Holofernes and Nathaniel have recruited Armado and the other villagers to perform *The Nine Worthies* for the courts of Navarre and France both of which agree to see the play which they take great delight in deprecating. The horseplay is interrupted by the arrival of Marcade a French noble with the news that the princess's father is dead. Because of this the princess and her retinue must return to France immediately. At this prospect the Navarrians proclaim that their loves are true despite their frivolous behaviour. Each of the ladies sets their respective lords a yearlong task to prove their faithfulness, if completed they will be married. Just before the French depart Armado returns and announces that he will work as a ploughman for three years for love of Jaquenetta and asks to complete the entertainment that had been interrupted with a dialogue written by two learned men between the Owl and the Cuckoo; the former representing winter the latter spring. This song is sung and the play ends on a bitter-sweet note.

CAST LISTS AND CREDITS

Cast lists and credits

Stage

Actor	A Midsummer Night's Dream	Hamlet	Love's Labour's Lost
DAVID AJALA	Cobweb	Reynaldo	Lord
SAM ALEXANDER	Philostrate	Rosencrantz	Dumaine
EDWARD BENNETT	Demetrius	Laertes	King of Navarre
RICKY CHAMP	Snout	Lucianus	Costard
EWEN CUMMINS	Snug	Barnardo	Dull
ROBERT CURTIS	Theseus	Francisco	Forester
TOM DAVEY	Lysander	Guildenstern	Longaville
PETER DE JERSEY	Oberon	Horatio	
JOE DIXON	Bottom		Armado
PENNY DOWNIE		Gertrude	
KATHRYN DRYSDALE	Hermia		Katherine
SAMUEL DUTTON	Mustardseed	Court Attendant	Lord
OLIVER FORD-DAVIES		Polonius	Holofernes
RYAN GAGE	Flute	Osric	Lord
MARIAH GALE	First Fairy	Ophelia	Princess of France
MARK HADFIELD	Puck	Gravedigger	Boyet
ANDREA HARRIS	Titania	Cornelia	Lady
JIM HOOPER	Starveling	Priest	Sir Nathaniel
KEITH OSBORN	Egeus	Marcellus	Marcade
RODERICK SMITH	Quince	Captain	Understudy (Holofernes)
NINA SOSANYA			Rosaline
RIANN STEELE	Hippolyta	Lady-in-Waiting	Jaquenetta
PATRICK STEWART		Claudius/Ghost	
DAVID TENNANT		Hamlet	Berowne
ZOE THORNE	Moth	Page	Moth
NATALIE WALTER	Helena		Maria
JOHN WOODVINE		Player King	

Director	Gregory Doran
Designers	Francis O'Connor (*Dream, Love's*)
	Robert Jones (*Hamlet*)
	Original production of Dream *designed by Stephen Brimson Lewis*
Costume Designer	Katrina Lindsay (*Love's*)
Lighting Designer	Tim Mitchell
Composer	Paul Englishby
Sound	Martin Slavin (*Dream, Love's*)
	Jeremy Dunn assisted by Martin Slavin (*Hamlet*)
Music Directors	Julian Winn (*Dream*)
	John Woolf (*Hamlet*)
	Bruce O'Neil (*Love's*)
	James Dodgson (*Hamlet*, London)
Movement Director	Michael Ashcroft
Fight Director	Terry King
Assistant Director	Cressida Brown